Implementation for Sustainability

Lessons from Integrated Rural Development

Implementation for Sustainability

Lessons from Integrated Rural Development

BY

George Honadle and Jerry VanSant

KUMARIAN PRESS

Cover design by
Marilyn Penrod

Library of Congress Cataloging in Publication Data

Honadle, George.
   Implementation for sustainability.

   (Library of management for development)
   Includes bibliographies and index.
   1. Rural development projects—Developing countries—
Management. 2. Rural development projects—Developing
countries—Management—Case studies. I. VanSant,
Jerry. II. Title. III. Series.
HD1417.H66   1985   338.9'0068   85-12538
ISBN: 0-931816-33-5
ISBN: 0-931816-47-5

CONTENTS

TABLES AND FIGURES

Preface

From 1978 to 1984, Development Alternatives, Inc. (DAI) and the Research Triangle Institute (RTI) carried out field work aimed at using development administration and organizational development skills to improve the implementation of 24 integrated rural development projects in Asia, Africa, Latin America, and the Caribbean.[1] This volume builds on the field reports, working papers, and published articles generated from that field work. The central foundation for the conclusions rests on experience with these projects.

Selection of the projects was not based on a rigorous sample design, although a conscious attempt was made to develop recurring work with a set of projects that was representative in terms of location, size, scope, substance, and stage of implementation. Other factors affecting the choice of sites included demand from the field for management- and organization-related technical assistance, the interests of the DAI and RTI professional staff who were involved and the expected significance of the proposed field work.

Our mandate was to combine engagement with reflection, providing direct assistance to the field while gleaning lessons that could be generalized from the field experience. In a sense, our task was research, but it quickly became apparent that we would have difficulty obtaining invitations to visit project sites just to study how work was organized and managed.

Since no lessons could be examined without field access, the first task was to get on site and demonstrate that the application of development administration and organizational development skills could be helpful. As a result, the overlay of a rigorous research design on barely comparable work assignments was discarded. That approach was seen as a barrier both to field access and to learning since questions of how to quantify predetermined variables could easily dominate questions of how to solve real problems and how to identify important dimensions that lay outside initial hypotheses.

In the first year of the field work, the emphasis was therefore on access to, and observation of, a range of integrated rural development projects in several countries that could lead to multiple follow-up visits. Subsequently, the focus moved to providing recurrent assistance in accordance with scopes of work jointly developed by field project staff and proposed DAI/RTI teams.

Assignments ranged from policy or sector studies (in Botswana, Egypt, and Thailand) to assistance in the design of an information system (in Nepal), to conducting a six-month pilot project in decentralized planning and management (in Egypt), to direct assistance in improving field management (in Jamaica, Liberia, Niger, and the Philippines), to assessing and improving implementation strategies (in Cameroon, Ecuador, Pakistan, Indonesia, Sudan, Tanzania, and Thailand) to program organization and design (in Panama, Ecuador, Cameroon, and Pakistan). Altogether, the field work included most dimensions of organization and management. The wide range of country situations underscored the diversity of development environments while illustrating how often a few intractable problems tend to reappear.

By 1980, the demand for field assistance was so great that all requests could not be met. Resources were then concentrated to allow multiple visits to a select group of field efforts. These efforts were chosen to represent the range of organizational strategies in integrated rural development, but the emphasis was still on field assistance, combined with an unobtrusive attempt to develop comparative knowledge.

More than 40 staff members of DAI and RTI carried out field work, using multidisciplinary teams on short-term visits to a project site. Multiple visits provided continuity and enabled the visitors to see how their contributions supported local efforts over time. The team was depicted as part of the overall management effort—the equivalent of adding an outside task force to assist the field staff to accomplish their objectives. Research was not emphasized. Instead, the intent was to forge informal links and build a shared commitment to helping the field staff deal with their own problems as they perceived them. As a result, the short-term teams gained a deep appreciation for the context in which project implementers operate. Indeed, one result of this practice was to question the common modes of applying technical assistance.

An attempt was also made to have members of short-term teams share their experiences with other teams and with field staff. In fact, team members were made familiar with the common problems associated with implementation so that parallel data and experiences could be brought to bear on the issues at hand.[2] This approach also helped to mold field visits as joint learning missions rather than merely as technology transfer efforts.

Although this work began in 1978, the staff, including the authors, had other experience in both short- and long-term development assistance, much of it with the same projects or in the same areas as the immediate field experiences reported here. As a result, this book incorporates documented and undocumented experience that goes beyond the project assistance provided as part of the 1978–84 effort. Discussion of the Lilongwe and Karonga projects in Malawi, for example, is based on one author's experience there in 1967–70, as well as subsequent trips in 1980 and 1982. But the importance of the lessons to the topic at hand dictated that these projects be included. Similarly, the other author worked with the Provincial Area Development Program in Indonesia over a six-year period. Only a portion of that work was funded under the study reported here, but the lessons of broader involvement with the project are, of course, included in the observations. A review of 21 United States Agency for International Development-assisted projects[3] plus an extensive review of the management literature[4] also supplemented the field work and extended the data base for this discussion. Appendix A to this book lists the projects and the nature of the field work performed for each of them and Appendix B comprises an overview of the characteristics of the projects examined in the review cited above.

Because the field work was designed to respond to field needs, no single pre-established research design was applied to all the projects. But this fact should not cause the book to be dismissed as based on poor or noncomparable evidence. An understanding of implementation dynamics requires access to information about informal management practices that is acquired only through direct engagement over time. Thus, personal familiarity with the flow of events led to a choice of illustrations weighted toward the authors' direct experience. But these anecdotes are used to illustrate points that the authors and their colleagues found applicable in a wide range of settings.

The relationships found between management practices or organizational structures, on the one hand, and project or program outcomes, on the other, are not expressed in quantitative terms. This might have been done, but the resulting false precision would have been more protective than informative. Rather than taking this route, we chose to let the descriptions of management processes and critical incidents stand on their own, but within an analytic framework. Those who place their faith in regression coefficients will find no solace here; for those who have struggled through the messy world of project implementation, however, we hope the observations will ring true and the lessons will provide practical guidance.

Although the focus of this analysis is on integrated rural development, some of the projects were narrower in functional or geographic scope than many would associate with that term. But no matter how the boundaries of integrated rural development itself are defined, we believe that the lessons learned from the set of projects underlying this book are applicable to rural development in general. And so this experience is presented in the hope that it will be of service to those on the front lines of development implementation as well as to others who want to understand the role of organization and management in turning development projects into self-sustaining improvements in local settings.

Notes

1. This work was supported by what is now the Agency for International Development's Office of Rural and Institutional Development, Bureau of Science and Technology, through contract no. 936-5300, "The Organization and Administration of Integrated Rural Development."

2. See Elliott R. Morss and David D. Gow, *Integrated Rural Development: Nine Critical Implementation Problems*, IRD Research Note no. 1 (Washington, DC: Development Alternatives, Inc., 1981).

3. Paul R. Crawford, *Implementation Issues in Integrated Rural Development: A Review of 21 USAID Projects*, IRD Research Note no. 2 (Washington, DC: Development Alternatives, Inc., 1981).

4. George Honadle, Elliot R. Morss, Jerry VanSant, and David D. Gow, *Integrated Rural Development: Making It Work?* (Washington, DC: Development Alternatives, Inc., 1980).

Acknowledgments

This volume has its roots in a report prepared for the Office of Multisectoral Development, United States Agency for International Development. That report, "Integrated Rural Development: Making it Work?," was written in 1980 and provided a framework for examining a variety of rural development programs. Since that time, our thinking has undergone substantial change based on subsequent field experience as well as critical reflection on the issues raised in the earlier work. Accordingly, this book is a major departure from that report.

Nevertheless, we owe a great deal to three coauthors of the first report. David Gow, Elliott Morss, and Peter Weisel provided lasting substantive and stylistic contributions.

Numerous co-workers conducted field work, searched literature, or helped to produce materials that provide a basis for this volume. Among colleagues particularly involved in this effort were Thomas Armor, Tony Barclay, Jennifer Bremer, Earl Brown, John Buck, James Carney, Paul Crawford, John Hannah, Raymond Isely, Donald Jackson, Kenneth Koehn, Donald Mickelwait, Gene Owens, Roger Poulin, and Jerry Silverman.

Others who offered comments, criticisms, and guidance include James Lowenthal, Ronald Curtis, Derick Brinkerhoff, David Korten, John Cohen, Jerome French, Robert Shoemaker, Kenneth Kohrner, Mac Odell, Marcia Odell, Rudi Klauss, Samuel Hayes, Francis Lethem, William Siffin, Anne Hauge, Ed Connerly, Steven Franzel, Craig Olson, Gary Hansen, Marcus Ingle, and Thomas Carrol. Their reactions to the original report or subsequent revisions are appreciated.

A helpful role was played by Tjip Walker, who acted as sounding board during early stages and critiqued the final draft. Linda Robinson provided crucial support during the final stages of preparation. Finally, we thank Krishna Sondhi of Kumarian Press for her patience and support.

The assistance of all of those mentioned above is gratefully noted. As usual, responsibility for all errors of omission or commission, whether of fact or of conclusion, is retained by the authors. But more important than absolving others, who are named, from complicity in the weaknesses of the volume is crediting the unnamed with its strengths. The substance and orientation rest on shared experiences with local field officers, farmers, villagers, entrepreneurs, and civil servants in 19 developing countries. Many will see their perspectives and encounters presented here. Requests for anonymity have been honored, but our enduring debt to these partners in development must be emphasized. In many ways, this is their story.

George Honadle
Jerry VanSant

CHAPTER ONE

Linking Implementation and Sustainability

W hy do some development projects result in long-run improvements, whereas others introduce only a temporary change in local activity? Many people have asked this question and numerous answers have been offered. Recently, those answers have shifted away from purely strategic explanations toward an awareness of the crucial role of the tactical aspects of organization and management in project success. Sound schemes alone fail to induce development. When people and materials cannot be coordinated or when bureaucratic procedures block performance, good ideas deteriorate into bad experiences. The widespread occurrence of these events suggests that an important area of concern should be implementation.

But this raises another question—namely, implementation for what? It is difficult to assess the relative merits of different implementation strategies without identifying the objective of the implementation process. In fact, some observers question whether common success measures such as per capita income, roads, or food production are adequate to capture the essence of development. Temporary infusions of project resources often generate employment and income benefits that do not last beyond outside funding; roads can deteriorate rapidly if they are not maintained; and quick production jumps may benefit powerful landowners rather than poor farmers. These critiques of the development record emphasize the need to go beyond inventories of artifacts to encounter the need for changes in local capacities to make improvements self-sustaining. Thus, an analysis of implementation practices should be based on the contribution they make to sustainability.

Sustainability

It is important to define the meaning of sustainability. Previous literature on the subject of institution building has often equated success with the perpetuation of an organization.[1] That is, the recognizable continuation of a formal body, such as an institute of tropical agriculture, was considered a measure of success. In this book, however, success is not the perpetuation of an organization. Instead, it is the continuation of benefit flows to rural people with or without the programs or organizations that stimulated those benefits in the first place. The classic example is the farmer who learns about a new technology from an agriculture extension service and then is able to apply it successfully. Of course, the bottom line is that this application leads to enhanced production of marketable produce and that institutions exist that can refine the technology and maintain the higher production and income levels, but the original organizational channel that was used may no longer exist or no longer provide the needed services.

An organization may cease to exist because another body has assumed its functions. In fact, this is the explicit intention of many program designers who expect cooperatives or other local community organizations to take over a project's marketing operations. Conversely, some organizations stumble along well after the demand for their services has subsided. This is especially true of public sector units based on an unobtrusive line item in the national budget. The Philippines, for example, is dotted with empty low-profile organizations with distant origins. In some situations, success may result in the private sector providing marketing or input supply services originally started by a public sector intervention. Clearly, neither the form of an organization nor its survival may be equated with sustainability. If either is overemphasized, there is inadequate recognition that benefits continue or fail to continue as a result of what people actually do, within or without the initiating organization.

Looking at sustainability demonstrates a concern for what happens after a project terminates. The need for this emphasis is rooted in a development mode that relies on temporary projects using outside resources.

If development were a one-time procedure like a vaccination with a lifetime effectiveness there would be no reason to be concerned with sustainability. But development is not such a procedure. Simple infusions of outside resources rarely generate self-sustaining improvements in productivity and life quality.

For progress to be made in the practice of development, then, attention must be concentrated on the process of converting resources into development gains. The connection between implementation and sustained outcomes must be understood.

For the purpose of assessing this connection, the degree of sustainability may be considered as the percentage of project-initiated goods and services that is still delivered and maintained five years past the termination of donor resources, the continuation of local action stimulated by the project, and the generation of successor services and initiatives as a result of project-built local capacity. Ideally, this assessment would include a visit to each project site five years after its termination to determine the magnitude and nature of the inheritance left behind.

These visits did not take place. However, momentum resulting from successful practices often appeared capable of continuing past external funding. At the same time, it was possible to observe examples of disintegration that occurred before termination, making it unlikely that benefits would last even to the end of outside support. Although there is more certainty about failure than about success, tentative statements may be made about both and about the way particular implementation practices and design characteristics are related to each of them.

Characteristics of Integrated Rural Development

Integrated rural development (IRD) is usually understood to be a multisectoral, multifunctional development initiative placed in one or several different locations. Integration is basically a response to the judgment that the rural farmer's poverty stems from a host of problems requiring a package of coordinated responses—from health services to agricultural extension to credit and technology dissemination.[2] As a result of their relative size and complexity, most IRD projects are donor assisted and have had their conceptual origin with donors.

The IRD projects in this sample range from small community-based efforts by private voluntary organizations (PVOs) such as the Save the Children Federation, through area-based or district programs targeted on a few thousand hectares and a corresponding number of people, to large regional and national development programs. Projects studied for this book varied in budget from only $200,000 a year to more than $10 million yearly, such as Columbia's Integrated Rural Development Program. Generally the projects cluster around budgets of $2–3 million a year over a funding period of three to five years, although a recent trend is toward longer time horizons, sometimes up to 10 years. This great empirical variability usually goes unrecognized by those writing about IRD.[3]

The focus of these IRD projects also varies. Roads, clinics, literacy, land, irrigation, and livestock are typically emphasized. At the higher end of the budget range, IRD tends to involve a few social service components tacked on to a program of infrastructure development. Since most of the budget goes for the physical products, this facet overwhelms the attention of management and dominates the implementation process. Sometimes institutional development is an explicit objective, such as in the Provincial Area Development Program in Indonesia. Usually, however, the institutional element appears as the introduction of a cooperative or similar local organization to perform necessary project functions. Marketing, credit, labor mobilization, and irrigation system management are typical activities in which these organizations are engaged.

The development literature is moving toward more precise distinctions among rural development, agriculture development, and integrated rural development. The basis for this volume is not the literature however. It is instead based on field observation.

At first glance, the variation in the components, organizations, and objectives of these projects may seem contrary to this movement toward precision and clarity. But the combination of an agricultural production component with other service-oriented elements characterized all the field efforts.

Furthermore, our interest is in the organization and management of development programs in general, and the common patterns observed within this group of projects suggests that their variety is not a hindrance to this effort. IRD, as reflected in these field examples, provides an open window for looking at the organization and management of development initiatives encompassing a wide range of scope and substance.

In addition to scope and substance, the context in which IRD is implemented has significance for management and organizational choices. Common factors to consider are discussed below.

First, IRD projects often are located near international borders. When farm-gate prices are held low or when desired goods are more available on the other side, the proximity of these borders may result in the siphoning off of livestock or agricultural produce, such as crops intended for marketing through parastatal bodies. Borders may also be politically sensitive because of disagreements with neighboring states or illegal flows of immigrants.

Second, IRD projects that emphasize food production may occupy a particularly important position in a national policy setting that gives priority to providing cheap food for urban populations. As a result, the prices IRD participant farmers receive for their produce may be significantly higher than the depressed prices charged in nonproject settings.

Third, IRD projects frequently are situated in an area with a history of political disaffection toward the national government. This may be a region, tribal territory, or a district or municipality within an otherwise politically supportive area. Political opposition makes it difficult for project designers to understand local cultures or to design projects that are sociologically feasible.

Fourth, IRD projects often impose changes in the local authority structure by introducing temporary arrangements for project management and by using technical criteria to replace traditional patterns of decision making. IRD's significance as a penetration mechanism is seldom lost on local leaders. Many implementation problems arise from attempts by those who are losing control to slow down or reverse the process.

Fifth, IRD projects are often part of a process of decentralization by the national government. When these policies are stated, development of subnational capacity for project management is sometimes an explicit objective of the IRD effort.

Sixth, IRD projects are usually administratively complex. They impose heavy requirements for coordination on project staff with limited leverage over line ministries and other agencies whose cooperation is critical to a multisectoral effort.

These characteristics may be interrelated. For example, the establishment of an IRD effort based on irrigated rice production could be used simultaneously to seal a border, produce food, provide an increased government presence in an unruly region, and transfer land allocation authority from the village head to the new project management unit. At times, multiple objectives are mutually supportive. At other times, however, they can be contradictory. Thus, a project may use subsidies to induce growers to produce, risking a recurrent cost burden that constrains institutional development in the responsible agency. Or, the rhetoric of decentralization linked to an implicit attempt to gain greater control over the hinterlands may create distrust leading to unproductive local management behavior. Unfortunately, these situations occur frequently in rural development efforts.

Three points emerge from an awareness of these characteristics of IRD. First, formal statements of program objectives, the philosophy of IRD, or the technical dimensions of integrated approaches seldom adequately explain what worked or what did not and why.[4] Second, the process of IRD implementation often contains basic contradictions.[5] Among the most difficult is the tradeoff between immediate measurable results and capacity building in implementing agencies. This is no less true of the development enterprise in general; identifying these contradictions and their manifestations should help shed light on reasons why apparently sensible solutions seldom seem to make a difference.

Third, program failure is not primarily a result of lack of political will. Instead, it results, at least in part, from wills in conflict and the impact of this conflict on the organization and management of the development process. Examining experience with this process and suggesting ways to improve it constitute the tasks of this book.

Its primary focus is on organization and management factors and their effect on sustainability. Since IRD implementation obviously has a strong political dimension, politics are important too. Even sustainability has political overtones. Willingness to maintain a road, availability of funds to cover recurrent costs, adoption of appropriate technologies, and desirability of giving resources and power to subnational bodies all reflect political priorities.

At the same time, these issues are more than just political. Roads across deserts cost less than those across swamps, and sustaining the vitality of an organization in a place with no resource endowment is more difficult than keeping a well-placed organization, such as an irrigators' association, in business. Thus, improving the craft of rural development requires more than bemoaning political difficulty. It calls instead for a bolder approach that harnesses past experience and, recognizing both contradictions and uncertainties, directs that experience toward promising new pathways. But to do this, a framework is necessary to organize the experience.

A Conceptual Framework

There are many ways to look at the project implementation process. The choice of analytic perspective naturally influences the observer's judgments. This book suggests a conceptual framework that emphasizes the process of development and the importance of sustaining the benefits of that process.

Broadly stated, development projects involve the deliberate use of resources to achieve self-sustaining improvements in human well-being and capabilities. Project implementation is the process of transforming those resources to achieve that objective. Ideally, local demand for development should be the initiating factor for project activities. In reality, the impetus commonly comes from outside. In either case, the typical project pattern brings external inputs to a local situation to address welfare and capacity goals.

Implementation normally takes place within an organizational setting. For example, an irrigators' association manages labor, information, finances, and physical resources to give farmers a water supply, which helps increase rice yields and thus contributes to higher income levels. Similarly, integrated area development projects organize funds, facilities, equipment, and staff to train farmers in improved cultivation practices, leading to higher yields and greater incomes.

The changes that are sought are usually complex and uncertain as well as largely uncontrollable. Since individuals are unable to induce the changes single-handedly, organizations are needed to facilitate and manage them. Project management units, line ministries, political parties, cooperatives, formal village associations, and informal seasonal agricultural work groups are all examples of organized effort in the development process.

The jump from applying resources to obtaining sustained welfare improvements, however, is a great one. In fact, if intermediate stages are not identified, this jump remains little more than a leap of faith. Fortunately, a common pattern emerges from development experience. First, the resources are used to provide some type of goods or services. Second, people respond by using (or ignoring) the services. If the response is positive and produces benefits that can be sustained, the result is development.

Thus, two intermediate objectives may be inserted between the application of resources and the achievement of sustained development. The first one is the delivery of goods and services, and the second is people's responses to them. This sequence of objectives is displayed in Figure 1.

Figure 1
IMPLEMENTATION AS SEQUENTIAL OBJECTIVES

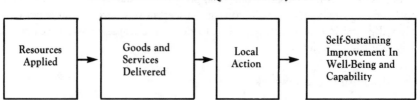

Implementation, then, is the process of managing the achievement of sequential objectives. For example, delays in road construction plague many rural development schemes and block the conversion of resources into the delivery of a good, such as improved market access. When farmers refuse to adopt new technologies, agricultural extension agents experience firsthand a nonresponse. When farmers do try new methods but yields or prices fall, they suffer from the failure of their response to lead to improved well-being.

Moreover, the sustainability of an initiative has important human implications. The inability to maintain a road not only leads to physical decay, but also erodes human confidence and undermines the credibility of future development initiatives. Similarly, when a farmer has taken a risk and switched to production practices requiring fertilizers, tools, pesticides, and new work patterns, and these inputs later prove unavailable or inappropriate, he or she feels betrayed or exploited. This experience is likely to constrain that farmer's subsequent adoption of extension advice. Thus, the links between the sequential objectives must be forged in ways that improve chances for sustainability.

The key dimension of Figure 1 is represented by the arrows—that is, the process of achieving the sequence of objectives. This is where organization and management can make a difference since they are major components of the deliberate effort to turn targets into accomplishments. Moreover, different implementation processes can have different effects on sustainability. Since this is the primary concern of this book, it will guide the discussion of alternative tactics for organizing and managing rural development programs.

The logic of the conceptual framework posits a flow through time, from left to right, from one objective to the next in the sequence—it is impossible to deliver services without human or financial resources or to use services before they exist. Nevertheless, the latter stages of the sequence—local response and benefit sustainability—must be considered when implementing the earlier stages. For example, beneficiaries will not use new services if they expect that their welfare, as they define it, will decrease as a result of this use. Different projects attempt to do different things, but all require effective linkages between resources, service delivery, local response, and sustainable benefit flows. Measuring the success of a project in terms of impact essentially means assessing the quality of these linkages.

This perspective is necessary to ensure that each linkage is managed in ways that lead to self-sustaining impact. Not only what is accomplished but also how it is done is important. Project managers must consider the possibility that the processes they use to apply resources, deliver goods and services, and evoke response will, in fact, lower the possibility that these processes will continue after the project has ended. Without a conscious effort to focus on post-project issues, a shortsighted service emphasis tends to dominate decisions. This problem is exacerbated by the contradictions and nonlinear relationships that characterize interactions among the various elements in this seemingly simple sequence. The contradictions are explored in greater detail below.

A Sequence of Contradictions

Goods or services must be delivered for people to use them. What is needed to deliver them, however, may be the very thing that precludes their use. If management authority is fragmented, for example, coordinated service delivery is made difficult. Yet the positive response of villagers is made more likely by their participation in program decisions—an approach that diffuses authority. This contradiction is inherent in the implementation process. One stage requires concentrated authority, whereas another calls for shared authority.

A second contradiction emerges in discussions of the relative merits of using temporary as opposed to permanent organizations to implement development projects. Temporary units are good at physical construction such as building roads, ports, clinics, or other facilities, but they usually are not structured to provide permanent funding and management. Thus, a focus on long-term sustainability supports the use of permanent institutions. At the same time, the seeming impossibility of getting anything done inside existing institutions drives project designers toward temporary task forces or management units. If nothing is started, there is nothing to sustain.

Other occurrences that generate contradictions are:

- Inaccurate statements or promises by politicians create false expectations of immediate benefits rather than an understanding of longer-term development processes.
- Foreign donors prefer financing new projects to underwriting recurrent costs of past initiatives or carrying earlier efforts to the point where they become viable.
- Promised host country resources are not forthcoming, either because the resource level required is unreasonable or because the government chooses not to provide them, but staff is nonetheless exhorted to work harder.
- Project staff pay little attention to sustainability issues as a result of pressures for immediate delivery of goods and services.
- Local action in the form of ongoing participation, resource commitment, or other appropriate response to project initiatives is absent because the emphasis on staff performance relegates secondary status to beneficiary initiative.
- Low rates of financial return or insufficient cash flow render income-producing activities untenable while new organizations are expected to assume responsibility for performing these activities.
- Project satellite organizations are often established to control beneficiary behavior while they are expected to evolve into mechanisms for representing beneficiary interests.

These and other contradictions will be examined in later chapters. In some cases, resolutions will be offered; in others, there are none. In all instances, however, the overriding objective of sustainability will be employed to assess the relative merits of alternative solutions within the context of rural development management.

The Context of Rural Development Management

The experience base for this book encompasses a time span of five years in the late 1970s and early 1980s. Thus, it is not immune from the particular myths and insights or the global political economy of that time. Much the same may be said of IRD itself, which emerged from the experience of the late 1960s and early 1970s.

In the 1960s, Third World development was viewed largely as a problem of national planning. Borrowing from a European model of technocratic elites determining optimum resource allocation to achieve economic objectives, such as industrial development and import substitution, governments gave major priority to comprehensive national plans. First stages emphasized physical infrastructure as the prerequisite for generating engines of growth. Roads, ports, and hydroelectric projects were to establish linkages that would generate production gains and widespread income benefits.[6]

As equity concerns emerged in the early 1970s, decentralization and a focus on poverty gained in importance.[7] Planning descended from its national focus to emphasize subnational areas that could act as growth poles.[8] Integration at this level reflected a balanced growth strategy writ small—infrastructure, agricultural production, cottage industry, education, health services, and employment generation made up a package to alleviate poverty in selected areas. When this package was combined with the discrete project approach to development investment applied in rural areas, the strategy was often called IRD.

Most of the IRD projects discussed in this book had their roots in a transition period, when comprehensive blueprints for development evolved from a concern with building physical infrastructure to an emphasis on benefiting the poorest segments of the population in selected geographic areas. The transitional environment surrounding the conception of these projects should be kept in mind when examining contradictions in the implementation experience and the difficulty of achieving sustainability. This environment promoted contradictory designs—rhetoric emphasized alleviating poverty, but resources were spent on capital-intensive physical infrastructure; goals stressed the process of institutional development and local capacity building, but immediate targets and donor evaluations focused on physical production and resource disbursement. Managers were often given conflicting tasks, but not the means to resolve the conflicts. The result was a preoccupation with project service delivery at the expense of adequate consideration of post-project viability. It is necessary to examine the various approaches taken to service delivery to understand how this happened.

Notes

1. Most of that literature is summarized in Melvin G. Blase, *Institution Building: A Source Book* (East Lansing, MI: MUCIA, 1973); and in Joseph W. Eaton, ed., *Institution Building and Development: From Concepts to Application* (Beverly Hills, CA: SAGE Publications, 1972).

2. Coralie Bryant and Louise White, *Managing Development in the Third World* (Boulder, CO: Westview Press, 1982), 290.

3. A recent example of this failing is Vernon W. Ruttan, "Integrated Rural Development Programmes: A Historical Perspective," *World Development* 12, no. 4 (1984): 393–401.

4. This point is made in Robert Chambers, "Rapid Rural Appraisal: Rationale and Repertoire," *Public Administration and Development* 1, no. 2 (1981): 95–106; and in George Honadle, "Rapid Reconnaissance for Development Administration: Mapping and Moulding Organizational Landscapes," *World Development* 10, no. 8 (1982): 633–649.

5. The first one to identify the conceptual confusion that preceded the empirical variation was John M. Cohen. See "Integrated Rural Development: Cleaning Out the Underbrush," *Sociologia Ruralis* 20 (1980): 195–212. This article is highly recommended.

6. Albert O. Hirschman, *The Strategy of Economic Development* (New Haven, CT: Yale University Press, 1958).

7. Edgar Owens and Robert Shaw, *Development Reconsidered* (Lexington, KY: D.C. Heath and Co., 1972).

8. See E. A. J. Johnson, *The Organization of Space in Developing Countries* (Cambridge, MA: Harvard University Press, 1970); and Dennis A. Rondinelli and Kenneth Ruddle, *Urbanization and Rural Development: A Spatial Policy for Equitable Growth* (New York: Praeger, 1978).

CHAPTER TWO

Delivering Goods and Services

M any observers of development have rightly emphasized the necessity for project and government agency staff to view their role as responding to the needs of villagers rather than just expecting the villagers to follow their overtures, advice, or direction. Although this attitude is commendable, it does not go far enough. For staff to respond effectively to villager needs invariably requires the staff to produce some combination of goods and services. This is no less true for a solitary community development worker than for a large and complex program. But as soon as the effort exceeds the ability of a single person to carry it out, the activities of those involved must be organized and managed.

Two of the first tasks that development managers confront are to obtain the promised funds and then turn them into services, such as advice, labor, or information, or into goods such as medicine, roads, buildings, or fertilizer. Experience with IRD, however, has been that host country ministries of finance are reluctant or, at least, slow to part with promised funds because of endemic shortages and competing demands. A major initial task, therefore, is simply to extract resources. Delays with the Provincial Area Development Program (PDP) in Indonesia, the Bula-Minalabac Integrated Area Development Project in the Philippines, and the Lofa County Integrated Agricultural Development Project in Liberia suggest that the problem is widespread, possibly even universal. Until funds are released, staff cannot be hired; until staff are working, roads will not be built, research will not be conducted, and extension programs will not operate. In short, nothing will be delivered.

Typical program designs add to the difficulties by spreading the control of resources among several parties. For example, in the Second Integrated Rural Development Project (IRDP II) in Jamaica, deployment of road-building equipment was controlled not by project managers but by the Ministry of Works. The same was true of Liberia's Bong County Integrated Agricultural Development Project. Coordination and timely action were thus made more difficult. Dual accountability of key field personnel to multiple agencies in the Philippines and Indonesia had similar effects.

Parceling out resources among various actors while expecting them to come together in the harmonious application of those resources toward a common objective is unrealistic. Based on project design and implementation experience in many countries, one study has called for a concentration of management authority and resource control to improve implementation of area-based projects.[1] The study also recognizes the political dimension of implementation and consequently does not assume that the problem is merely one of making resources available and then letting the experts do their jobs. Instead, it stresses the importance of considering organizational alternatives.

Organizational Alternatives

The choice of organizational configuration for implementing a rural development initiative results from pressures and conditions related to three factors: the technology to be employed, the ideas and strategies currently in vogue in the donor organization, and the political dynamics and capacities within various segments of the recipient country's governmental structure. The most common mechanism used in IRD programs has been the independent project management unit (PMU). Other options are to work through national line ministries such as agriculture or natural resources, employ new or existing national-level units such as parastatals or coordinating committees, or use provincial or regional governments. Each organizational alternative is discussed below in terms of the pressures leading to its use and its record based on observed implementation experience. A fifth option, the use of private voluntary organizations (PVOs), such as the Save the Children Federation or the Institute for Rural Reconstruction, also is considered.

Project Management Units

Infrastructure projects throughout the world use engineering field offices employing a temporary cadre of professionals and laborers to build a product according to a blueprint. These are called project management offices (PMOs) and are similar to the PMU noted above. The PMO may be a temporary task force within a private contracting organization or a roving unit within a public sector organization such as an army corps of engineers. In either case, the PMO is familiar to engineers in both high- and low-income countries as a task-oriented organizational mechanism with a high potential for getting jobs done. Among the reasons for its success are clear standards and procedures, task similarity, and organizational loyalty.

When confronted with the task of inducing rural development through the provision of basic infrastructural goods and services, planners often borrowed this approach from the engineering fraternity. After all, if rural development is essentially a technical problem, the best way to attack it is to draw good blue-prints and then give autonomous, technically oriented cadres the job of imple-menting them. This was a common mechanism for reducing political interference and bureaucratic red tape to a minimum to get a job done quickly. Moreover, the temporary nature of the unit meant that it was outside civil service regulations and thus could pay attractive salaries, ensuring that top-flight staff were recruited. It was also not a threat to the careers of line agency employees.

Since many IRD projects are infrastructure oriented and viewed by donors as investments to generate monetary return to the local economy, donors adopted the PMU as the preferred style of organization. Moreover, in the 1960s many national regimes in'developing countries sought ways to bring under their control the bureaucratic apparatus they had inherited from their colonial masters. PMUs provided a means to concentrate decision making, bypassing a bureaucracy viewed with suspicion, while bringing a high-visibility benefit to rural areas. Thus, a combination of technical and political considerations promoted the PMU strategy.

In addition, intellectual currents contained themes consistent with the use of PMUs. Discussions of dual economies and institution building, for example, emphasized the need to build enclaves to pursue technical and developmental objectives.[2] At the same time, a participatory, anti-bureaucratic and bottom-up perspective permeated the essentially top-down experience of the field of develop-ment administration.[3] The PMU fit well into this schizoid environment—a temporary enclave could be used to stimulate change without imposing a new bureaucratic burden on rural people. At last, the withering away of organizations could be achieved. And all this could be done while decision-making authority was moved closer to the field of action. Thus, PMUs became a dominant mecha-nism for the implementation of rural development.

But two hidden factors emerged to derail the lofty expectations for PMUs in IRD. First, an integrated focus often led to a PMU sharing its authority with another organization that had greater power and resources in one of the sectors the program addressed. For example, the PMUs of both the Lofa County project in Liberia and IRDP II in Jamaica relied on ministries of public works to build the roads that the project required. This situation resulted in uncoordinated and undelivered infrastructure and services. Second, the inability of PMUs to assume the recurrent costs of the activities they had begun became an apparent threat to project sustainability.

In reaction to this problem, strategies were devised to use PMUs as vectors of innovation and to overcome the sustainability problem. One approach was to create project-initiated satellite organizations with beneficiary members as the inheritors of PMU functions. Examples of this approach include the cooperatives promulgated by the Lofa and Bong projects in Liberia, the development commit-tees of IRDP II in Jamaica, and the irrigator associations and compact farms characteristic of IRD efforts emphasizing rice production, such as the integrated area projects in the Bicol region of the Philippines.

A second strategy was either to merge the PMU with a line ministry or to create a new ministry out of a cluster of area-based PMUs. The Lilongwe Land Development Project (LLDP) in Malawi was long heralded as an example of successful IRD.[4] In terms of the delivery of goods and services, this reputation was well deserved. Authority was concentrated in the PMU, and participation of beneficiaries was above average. Although not perfect, the PMU worked.

The success story did not end there. With the establishment of agricultural development divisions as the basic units within the Ministry of Agriculture, LLDP, or LADD as it is now called, became permanently institutionalized. LADD thus became the world's first perpetual PMU, or did it?

In this case, the distinction between sustainability and organizational perpetuation is important. LADD has not become self-sustaining. Instead, the project has entered a new stage in which recurrent costs are assumed by the donor, in this case the World Bank. What at first appears to be successful is, in fact, little more than dependence on a camouflaged crutch.

The other tactic, building a permanent ministry from a group of PMUs, has fared no better. This tactic was tried in Liberia in the mid-1970s. At that time, the Liberian institutional environment was characterized by onerous financial management procedures such as centralized purchasing, rigid preaudits, a salary payment system that immobilized field staff, and delays of up to six months for the most routine actions.[5] To avoid this administrative obstacle course, donor-supported rural development projects used PMUs to bypass the system.

In 1975, a coalition of donor staff and Liberians supported the creation of a rural development authority. Their plan was to reduce the authority of line ministries by combining rural development functions under county-level PMUs and then aggregating them into the equivalent of a ministry of rural development. The idea was twofold: first, to concentrate authority at the county level in a new unit that avoided the stasis of the larger system; second, to create a national-level entity to represent a rural development focus in the corridors of power.

Serious opposition to this approach was mounted, and the rural development authority was defeated. Instead, a new cadre of assistant county superintendents for rural development was created. This left the existing structure intact and signaled a victory for the line ministries.[6]

As long as it lasted, the PMU strategy did prove superior to line agencies at delivering goods and services to Liberian villagers. In addition, the autonomy of the PMU allowed it to continue to function with only minor disruptions during a period of political upheaval. But attempts to institutionalize the PMU failed.

Experience elsewhere supports these cases. Although PMUs have a strong record in converting resources into goods and services, they have a poor history of ensuring the continuation of lasting benefits beyond the end of donor financing. In recognition of this finding, the World Bank, long associated with the PMU strategy, has virtually abandoned it.

Subnational Government Bodies

The second most common organizational placement strategy is to use a provincial or regional government unit as the host for an IRD program. Examples of this approach include the Arusha Planning and Village Development Project in Tanzania and PDP in Indonesia. These efforts, typical of this model, focus on building the planning capacity of the host organizations by implementing a multisectoral array of subprojects and using that experience as a learning tool. Thus, a characteristic of this version of IRD is to reject the planning/implementation dichotomy and instead foster a learning-by-doing attitude toward rural development.

The significance of the resources these programs introduced varied in relation to pre-existing local programs. The Arusha project was the major activity in a region with a low population and a poor resource endowment. PDP, however, was one among many government activities, and, in Java at least, the resources it controlled represented a more marginal contribution. These differences in relative resources can strongly affect the capacity of a project to generate coordination and exercise effective management control over its activities.

A shared element of projects using subnational bodies is a commitment to some form of decentralization. In fact, this focus reflected a mid-1970s trend in Africa and Asia that involved donors directly in local government projects similar to earlier patterns of donor investment in Latin America.[7]

Projects supporting decentralization are increasingly common. But decentralization is no panacea for implementation problems or sustainability needs. Often, devolution of authority is resisted by those who will receive it. A distrust of decentralization is common among those who fear that they will not be given adequate resources to do the job and that the resulting failure will be blamed on them. In other cases, decentralization provides low-level officials with a means of self-aggrandizement at the expense of the local poor.

There are tradeoffs between centralized and decentralized decision making, many of which are frequently manifested in field experience. A centralized decision structure, for example, tends to overload formal communication systems and requires more infrastructure and resources than does a decentralized structure. Decentralized structures, in contrast, often require more elaborate informal channels.

Some tradeoffs are less clear. Research suggests, for example, that top-level administrators are better than junior staff at making decisions about linkages with outside organizations. Other studies conclude that a combination of decentralization decisions and multiple communication channels facilitates interorganizational cooperation.[8] The strengths and weaknesses of centralization and decentralization are summarized in Table 1.

The success of IRD projects using a decentralized approach varies greatly. Key factors appear to be:

- The degree of central government commitment to decentralization;
- The stage of decentralization (the beginning is more difficult);
- The project's strength in relation to predator organizations in the environment; and
- Pre-existing local capacities and the project's ability to build on them.

National Line Ministries

The third placement option is to give implementation responsibility to a national functional line agency, such as the ministry of agriculture. Since a line ministry is usually sector-specific, this placement often requires attaching personnel or units from other ministries to provide an integrated focus.

A prime example of this option occurs in the Bicol River basin of the Philippines, where a lead line agency model is used as the primary field-level implementation mechanism. Each area-based IRD project is placed under one of the national line agencies, such as the National Irrigation Administration for the Libmanan-Cabusao Integrated Area Development Project, the Ministry of Agrarian Reform for the Bula-Minalabac project, and the Bureau of Forest Development for the Buhi-Lalo Integrated Area Development Project. The choice of implementing organization is based on a predominant technical capability to address each project's particular needs. Moreover, a rotation pattern is established to ensure that a range of ministries will receive their turn.

The project-level operations are more complicated than they first seem, however. To ensure the multisectoral focus, staff are borrowed from other agencies. The Libmanan-Cabusao project, for example, has people attached to it from the Ministry of Local Government and Community Development; the Ministry of Agrarian Reform; and the Ministry of Agriculture's Bureaus of Agricultural Extension, Plant Industry, and Animal Industry. The implementing unit itself, however, is within the National Irrigation Administration. The 2,000-hectare project area is located in two municipalities, and the borrowed personnel are expected to carry out their respective agencies' missions in the locality as well as to engage in project activities. Thus, they serve two masters.

To prevent the two masters from pulling in opposite directions, coordinating committees are established. These committees are expected to resolve differences in priorities between the needs of the project and the programs of cooperating line agencies. In addition, team-building workshops and monetary incentives are used to sway the loyalties of the borrowed staff toward the project. Yet everyone knows that career advancement lies within the mother agency and not the project. Thus, at the field level the use of a line agency to execute a multisectoral effort becomes a complex affair.

TABLE 1

Strengths and Weaknesses of Centralization and Decentralization

	CENTRALIZATION	DECENTRALIZATION
STRENGTHS	• Increases speed of decisions with routine decisions and certain technologies • Allows control over incentive system in local organization and linked organizations • Raises probability that a controversial policy will be implemented • If an organization is both autocratic and centralized, change can be readily introduced • Top-level administrators have longer tenure, and decisions made by them about linkages with other organizations tend to produce more valuable interactions • Improves high-level morale and initiatives	• Increases speed of non-routine decisions and uncertain technologies • Participative, decentralized, and autonomous organizations are more productive, efficient, and satisfying • Decentralized decision making and multiple communication channels facilitate interorganizational cooperation • Although the direct power in the hands of national leaders is reduced, decentralization increases their ability to guide society by creating more communication links within it • Improves low-level morale and initiative • Facilitates client participation
WEAKNESSES	• Overloads communication systems and requires more infrastructure and resources than a decentralized system to produce decisions in a given time • Changes cannot be readily introduced into a bureaucratically centralized organization • Does not nourish new leadership • Sensitive to situations where national-level elite is not sympathetic to client group	• Requires highly developed informal communications channels • Without financial discretion at lower levels, decentralization will not work • Very difficult when inefficient disbursement systems exist • Often requires a project element to be designed specifically to improve low-level planning capability among those charged with implementation • Sensitive to situations where local-level elite is not sympathetic to client group

In fact, the organizational complexity of the Bicol model is far more detailed and sophisticated. For example, in the Libmanan-Cabusao project the main waterways were built by a private contractor responsible to the lead agency, whereas sublateral canals were built using local labor through community based groups organized through the project. A regional planning agency (the Bicol River Basin Development Program Office) monitored the implementation process, and within the lead agency, the project was seen as a PMU responsible to a national office of special projects. Thus, an organization chart that truly reflected the interorganizational relationships would test the skills of the most creative draftsman.

Often a seemingly simple organizational model with clear lines of authority and a permanent institutional status turned out to be complicated and confusing. In the Bicol region, the implementation arrangements simply mirrored the complexity of the institutional landscape of the Philippines. Experience elsewhere suggests that this pattern is common—even when a single agency or independent agencies are used, the need for coordination of IRD activities and the interdependent nature of institutional environments lead to rapid complication of organizational relationships.

A lesson, then, is to not be seduced by the simplicity of ideal types or the rush to simple single-agency solutions for the problems of environments that are far more subtle and interdependent than may immediately appear to outsiders. Field experience with lead line agencies indicates that they are handicapped in any attempt to deliver multisectoral mixes of goods and services. Seldom is any single organization so powerful and autonomous that jealousies, conflicts, and changing political winds cannot touch it.

National Integrated Rural Development Agencies

The fourth placement strategy is to use a national-level agency, such as a parastatal body or a national coordinating council, as the host for the program. Examples of this model include the Integrated Rural Development Program (DRI) in Columbia, INVIERNO in Nicaragua, PIDER in Mexico, the Rural Development Secretariat in Ecuador, and the Rural Sector Grant (RSG) in Botswana.

Just as the PMU strategy varies, so too the national IRD placement has different forms. One form is represented by Ecuador's Rural Development Secretariat, the other by Botswana's RSG. Both are top-down, but their approach to IRD differs.

The Rural Development Secretariat is in some ways the opposite of the PMU strategy followed in Liberia. Instead of beginning with field-level project units and then amalgamating them into a national-level authority, the approach was to establish the authority first and then to have it create an inventory of field activities. Although many coordinating and linking committees were to tie the new organization to existing ministries and bodies, the effect was to establish a parallel chain of responsibility with the potential to become a super ministry.

With changing political tides, however, the Rural Development Secretariat later lost much of its independence.

The establishment of a new agency for each new project has historically been a common way to do business in Latin America. Thus, regional variations preferences, and resource endowments may be expected to affect the specifics of the organizational alternatives for IRD.

One example of environmental factors influencing program design is RSG in Botswana. In a country of 750,000 people, a harsh physical environment, and limited human resources, creating additional institutions makes little sense. Instead, it is necessary to work through those struggling organizations that already exist.

RSG is a national-level IRD program with overall responsibility vested in a coordinating and supervising body placed in the Ministry of Finance and Development Planning. RSG is essentially a financing mechanism with a development fund that may be tapped by interested ministries with project proposals that meet the RSG criteria. Since the implementation of RSG-funded activities remains the responsibility of the functional line ministries, organizational arrangements at the field level are not RSG-specific. Instead, they are built on ministry and district operational units as well as on the planning and budgeting process and cycle of the government.

Annual reviews of the performance of subprojects in the previous year and those proposed for the upcoming year are held. These reviews take place during February and March, just before the government's fiscal year begins in April. Proposals, submitted as project memoranda, reach the review team through the normal planning process. Similarly, financing for RSG activities follows regular government channels. Thus, RSG exhibits an enhancement strategy, using existing structures and processes. Although it is top-down in its funding, its planning process is bottom-up, geared to the existing capacities in those ministries concerned with rural development.

National IRD agencies are often able to muster top-level support for a program, but they still remain among the least used organizational placements for IRD. Only where historical or other factors support their use are they likely to be found.

Private Voluntary Organizations

This placement strategy is a small-scale alternative to the more common large government programs. The implementer is a private organization using either public or private funds to bring development benefits to selected communities. This approach, which some see as community development in integrated garb, is carried out by projects such as the Ghanaian Rural Reconstruction Movement, the Guatemalan Rural Reconstruction Movement, and the Save the Children Federation's (SCF) Community Based Integrated Rural Development (CBIRD) Project in Indonesia.

The stated purpose of CBIRD, for example, is to improve the economic and social well-being of people living in project communities in Aceh Province. This improvement is defined in terms of increased income and improved health, education, and infrastructure leading to a more self-sufficient community. SCF describes its approach to community development as a process of working with villagers to help them acquire the motivation, confidence, and skills necessary to identify their problems and needs, set priorities, and eventually assume responsibility for decision making in the implementation of self-help projects.

This approach is not unique to SCF among PVOs. But its focus on process issues as opposed to traditional measures of success is unusually rigorous. For example, a women's sewing project may appear to be a typical income-producing initiative. SCF, however, sees this type of project as an opportunity to encourage women to organize around a common interest so that, as an organization, they may become involved in other community activities. SCF has learned from experience that from these organizations new projects and other initiatives often emerge.

An SCF Indonesia report states that in a project's early stages planning and management systems will be stressed over quality. Although project success is important, SCF emphasizes its desire to institutionalize new ways of doing things—providing rungs to help the poor climb the economic ladder.[9]

Although CBIRD is conceptually similar to many PVO programs in its community focus and emphasis on local participation, it is more comprehensive and better managed than most. It is also being institutionalized to an unusual degree through the links it has forged with formal government systems in Aceh. In general, it has magnified strengths and mitigated weaknesses common to PVO efforts. Its strengths include:

- Application of an organizational technology appropriate to local circumstances and with a direct return to participants;
- A rigorous effort to generate the widest possible local commitment to the new organizational pattern from prospective participants;
- A deliberate attempt to draw on local capacities for self-help;
- A policy of combining cooperation with local authorities (increasing to a maximum degree the access of the project system to beneficiaries) with inclusion of the poor in decision making (increasing to a maximum degree the access of beneficiaries to the project system); and
- A flexible planning approach that facilitates ongoing modification of project content in response to local needs.[10]

CBIRD's identifiable weaknesses include:

- The risk that a continuation of direct economic benefits will depend on future external financial support; and

- The project's dependence on the managerial and coordinating role played by a nonindigenous special project unit.

Large-scale area projects with a central planning focus usually lack the flexibility and sensitivity to local needs that underlie the strengths of a PVO project such as CBIRD. At the same time, the weaknesses noted above are common to most development projects; the key variables are the proximity and permanence of the source of funds and staff. Although PVOs tend to place staff in close proximity to project areas, PVO resources are neither indigenous nor permanent. To the extent that programs depend on supplementary donors (as SCF's depends on the United States Agency for International Development [AID]), the risks of resource interruption are increased. The strategies of the PVO approach must be institutionalized to reduce dependence on the PVO's leadership and resources. Few PVO programs have been as successful as SCF Indonesia in this regard, but the sustainability of CBIRD benefits when SCF departs still remains in doubt.

Thus, organizational placement influences the ability of a project to deliver goods and services to target populations. Although the PMU generally concentrates authority and gets the job done, it has not been successful at achieving self-sustaining impact. At the same time, each of the other placement strategies also has a mixed record. Table 2 displays some major tradeoffs among placement strategies. Ultimately, the choice of an implementing agency must depend on weighing the tradeoffs in the light of local conditions.

Organization is not the only determinant of implementation problems and successes. Management behavior is just as important. Moreover, organizational arrangements and management activity are not independent of each other.

Management Behavior

Field staff often complain that the project manager does not know how to manage. Although managers face difficult circumstances, the complaint is largely substantiated by observations of management behavior. In East Africa, for example, the expatriate chief of party for a technical assistance team was a technician without management skills. His performance as a manager was so poor that the team was perceived by local residents as a group of individuals pulling in opposite directions. In Asia, a project manager with only technical training was seen as grasping for assistance. Sensitive to the feelings of his staff that he did not know how to manage people, he read an outdated, low-quality management text based on industrial experience in a high-income country. Although this book was largely irrelevant, it was the only source available.

These examples seem to be the norm. Successful behavior has also been observed, however, and outstanding practices appear to be widely transferable.

TABLE 2

Alternative Implementing Organizations

Organization	Strengths	Weaknesses	IRD Experience
Project management units	Able to bypass onerous financial management systems	Is unable to pick up recurrent costs	The most common IRD implementing organization, the PMU, has proved to be highly effective for physical production, but it seldom succeeds in building local capacity to carry on. It exemplifies a bypass approach and generally avoids control-oriented administrative systems by staffing with expatriates and establishing independent administrative procedures. Theoretically, it provides a flexible temporary environment supportive of experimentation, but in fact this seldom happens.
	Often concentrates authority and delivers goods and services	Does not build capacity in permanent institutions	
	Is effective for infrastructure construction	Tends to try and perpetuate itself as an organization	
	Sometimes is insulated from political upheaval	Can be vulnerable to encroachment of line ministries	
	Can focus on specific renewable natural resources and technical areas	Competes with permanent institutions for scarce staff and usually offers highly paid temporary non-career positions	
	Usually provides donor with greater financial control		
Subnational government bodies	Can pick up recurrent costs as a permanent institution	Is difficult to use in small countries with poor human and institutional resource bases	This approach often uses subprojects as learning laboratories to build local capability. Planning and implementation are thus merged. Decentralization is usually stressed, but local officials are often suspicious of national intentions. Mixed signals can stifle implementation when rhetoric emphasizes learning, decentralization, and capacity building, but incentives, finances, and evaluations are geared to physical production targets.
	Builds capacity in permanent institutions	Often is vulnerable to encroachment of line ministries	
	Usually has strong horizontal linkages	Often serves local elites	
	Uses existing socio-political boundaries		

Organization	Strengths	Weaknesses	IRD Experience
	Often links planning and implementation	Multiple subprojects may be difficult to manage	
National line ministries	Can pick up recurrent costs as a permanent institution	Personnel attracted from other ministries create difficult management situation	When a multisectoral (IRD) job is given to a sectoral ministry, it usually leads to complex interorganizational relationships that are hard to manage. Although theoretically the approach provides clear lines of authority, in practice skilled managers are needed to contend with coordination difficulties. When the rhetoric of integration is mixed with multi-agency staff, a reluctance to set priorities and deal with different components sequentially tends to develop.
	Builds capacity in permanent institutions	Delegation of authority is often lacking	
	Has strong professional and technical orientation	May be hampered by national politics	
		May ignore local differences	
National IRD agencies	Can facilitate vertical integration of local and national objectives	Often has conflict with line ministries	This is largely a Latin American phenomenon, but a version has been used in low population countries of Africa. Parastatals with a multisectoral mandate are a variety of this model. Administrative redundancy and high conflict characterize one variant of this approach. A second pattern fills gaps but risks supporting technically weak subprojects.
	Can be structured to augment other institutions	May duplicate other institutions' functions	
	Can provide access to top-level decision makers	May ignore local differences	
		May be difficult to manage because of geographic dispersal of subprojects	

TABLE 2 (Continued)

Organization	Strengths	Weaknesses	IRD Experience
Private voluntary organizations	Can address micro-level needs and variations	Often lacks legitimacy and is viewed with suspicion	This is a contemporary multisectoral descendant of community development. It uses intermediate technologies and group dynamics as tools for self-reliance and sustainability. The integrated focus is at the community level rather than at the administrative level. In many cases, however, the PVO presence acts like a mini-PMU, with similar failings when the external resources are withdrawn.
	Can mobilize private resources	Has little leverage	
	Can stress capacity building at local levels	Is limited to small areas	
		Is sensitive to quality of personnel	
	Low profile insulates it from political battles and avoids predators	Has little access to top-level decision makers	
	Emphasizes informal processes and local role in decisions	Often has low technical quality	
		Often has little effect on formal system	

But when organizational forms are transplanted from industrial settings, they sometimes place limitations on the potential of even good management practices.

The Matrix Myth

IRD does not exist in a vacuum; it is susceptible to the political, economic, and intellectual trends of the times. One trend, based on the recommendations of U.S. and West European management consultants, was the use of a particularly complex and conflict-ridden model called a matrix organization.

The matrix style overlays multiple project teams or temporary task forces onto a permanent administrative structure. The highly successful National Aeronautics and Space Administration (NASA) is the prototype for this organizational model. The approach was touted as theoretically appropriate for population and rural development programs.[11] Some NASA characteristics, however, are seldom found where IRD is attempted. First, NASA was equipped with an enormous budget. Second, since NASA was staffed mainly by engineers, there was a commonality of world view that cannot be assumed in IRD projects. Third, NASA had an essential structural attribute—the program manager.

A program manager has the authority to resolve conflicts that arise between a project manager with responsibility for a set of actions in a particular location and a functional officer whose support is essential for project success. Without the program manager role, the complex, high-conflict matrix structure has little chance. The IRD experience suggests that this role almost never exists in a developing country project setting.

Since real responsibility is seldom delegated below the ministerial level, conflicts between project and line agency staff often must be resolved at the national level. This situation may turn minor field problems into hotly debated political issues that hinder implementation. Thus, the matrix style of formal organization may produce undesirable consequences when imposed on environments that are not ready to receive it. Even in places such as the Philippines— where a strong human resource base and familiarity with complex interorganizational dealings exist—matrix structures for project management have a spotty record.

In IRD, the matrix structure usually appears as a PMU embedded in a permanent institution, such as in the Bicol model discussed earlier. As in most development project settings, the result of a matrix was to escalate the need for management skills while forcing managers to overemphasize formal processes and make them unmanageable.

Informal Processes

Legalistic, overly formal, and rule-oriented management styles are major impediments to organizational performance. In fact, successful implementation of IRD projects is invariably related to a manager's ability to recognize and use informal procedures, relationships, agreements, and communication channels.

This observation seems to be valid in any culture or location. The IRD experience shows that behind-the-scenes relationships and maneuvers explain why things work or do not work. The ability to capture and guide informal dynamics also characterizes all outstanding managers.

Experience in Botswana, Egypt, Honduras, Indonesia, Jamaica, Liberia, Malawi, Niger, Panama, Sudan, Tanzania, and Thailand strongly supports this contention. An appreciation for the informal works in a wide range of cultural settings and in places with different resource endowments.

Two examples from IRD efforts in Luzon, Philippines, illustrate the point. The first example is at the program level; the second, at the field level. The director of a regional planning and coordinating unit successfully managed conflicts and obtained cooperation among the national line agencies operating in the region. He relied on informal discussions in non-business locations to create an atmosphere conducive to agreement and coordination, and to incorporate the views of important people who were concerned about the issues being considered. Significantly, the influence of these persons over project outcomes was based less on formal authority than on their ability to exert behind-the-scenes power. Common mechanisms included dinner meetings at village festivals and other traditional social encounters. When the unit's director was replaced by a military officer whose style was authoritarian and formalistic, the result was a decline in performance and morale and an increase in conflict.

The essence of an informal style is to encourage non-threatening involvement during the evolution of a decision to create a sense of joint responsibility among those whose cooperation is needed to implement it. When this kind of informal coalition is achieved, less resistance is encountered during implementation.

Transitional situations, such as a change in leadership, require a high sensitivity to informal agreements. Usually, leaders have implicit understandings with colleagues and those whose cooperation is needed to implement decisions. When a new actor violates those compacts, operations can come to a standstill until the misunderstanding is resolved.[12] Since turnover is common in IRD projects, recognizing the importance of informal dynamics is essential to avoid disrupting operations.

The second example shows how the clever use of informal access to resources allowed farmers to obtain what they wanted. The example also demonstrates the need for observers to delve into informal relationships to understand how things work. In 1977 a field-level information system was installed in an IRD project that was refurbishing and expanding an irrigation system, while building the capacity of an irrigators' association to operate the facility. Formal statements indicated that this information system was actively used; however, by 1979 its use had dropped considerably. This decline was partly the result of the area supervisor's limited commitment to beneficiary participation and partly because he had assumed other duties.

In 1981, however, there was a renewed use of the documents, especially the request-for-action form that allowed farmers to pinpoint problems and suggest action to alleviate them. The explanation for the information system's renewed use was twofold. First, the farmers liked the system and, having been exposed to it, wanted to use it. Second, the vice president of the irrigators' association had married a member of the project staff who worked in the section that controlled the duplicating machine and was responsible for reproducing and distributing information system forms. Thus, an informal channel was established to give the farmers access to the forms and to rejuvenate the sagging system.

The lesson these two examples provide is not just that managers should use informal arrangements and decision patterns. Project designs should not trap implementers in rigid blueprints that eliminate opportunities to incorporate and evolve informal processes.[13] Instead, a flexible and evolutionary approach is necessary.

The organizational placement of IRD efforts can also put a premium on a manager's ability to use informal channels and to create a sense of joint ownership of project activities. When interagency staff are attached to a lead line organization, both informal arrangements with their superiors and informal rewards for them are often needed so they will give priority to project demands. In this situation, interpersonal relationships are key to high performance.

Similarly, leadership and job satisfaction may be important for managing staff in a temporary PMU. Unless the organizational climate attracts loyalty and commitment, staff are likely to spend much of their tenure arranging for their post-project employment and establishing claims on their share of project assets.

Administrative Control

The acknowledgment that informal processes are important in IRD is consistent with a theme in the management literature. That is, management should not be equated with control.[14] At the same time, effective control over project assets must be maintained.

Although there is little romance in administrative detail, the importance of logistics, inventory control, and vehicle maintenance during implementation can loom large enough to eliminate any results that might be worth sustaining. It is tempting to blame such petty material concerns on the overcomplexity of large-scale IRD projects, and, indeed, they are vulnerale to this criticism. But unpaid staff and dangerous vehicles can threaten even the most alluring bottom-up efforts.

IRD projects throughout the developing world have found themselves held hostage to administrative and logistical trivia, including:

- Donor or host government preaudit practices that handicap implementers and introduce unnecessary delays;
- Chaotic filing systems that render retrieval of vital information difficult or even impossible;

- Conflict over the assignment, deployment, and maintenance of project vehicles;
- Diversion of project resources (human and financial) to other uses; and
- Commodity procurement characterized by inappropriate materials, no follow-up on orders, and delays sometimes exceeding two years.

Some of these problems are amenable to traditional solutions, such as training. For example, better systems for procurement follow-up, more open decision styles applied to vehicle deployment, and separation of custodial accountability and record keeping may be introduced through training and consultation.[15]

But counterproductive behavior cannot always be changed by training or communication. Sometimes environmental structures and incentives may be altered through incremental changes that are limited to the project itself. In other situations, however, the required changes would be massive and radical and, therefore, more difficult.[16]

The extreme reaction to this situation is to give total control to an outside party. This works well if the job is only construction. A case in point is the enlargement of the Selander Bridge in Dar es Salaam, Tanzania. A Japanese team using close supervision, seven-day work weeks, three shifts of local labor, and radio monitoring devices on vehicles, finished the bridge in less than three months—a job that might normally take up to two years in Tanzania.

Other examples, including some work done by major contracting firms in the Middle East, also fit this pattern. When a bypass approach is combined with tight administrative control, goods can be delivered. But the management of rural development is far different from that of infrastructure construction. As a result of the complexity of rural development and the concern for sustainability, neither the task nor the actual level of autonomy is likely to be so clear cut.

Managers who have some autonomy can often manipulate the incentive system within the project to avoid or lessen the effects of some of these problems. Postaudits of expenditures, for example, can replace preaudits, drawing down on periodic installments credited to expenditure categories. In other situations, mileage allowances for extension agents may be used to encourage vehicle maintenance. This approach was used successfully in the Arusha project in Tanzania.

There, the discouraging vehicle maintenance experience of the Maasai Range Management Project, which preceded the Arusha project, focused attention on the importance of this issue. Local labor laws did not encourage high performance by mechanics. Since the laws were a constraint, the solution was to build maintenance capacity outside the system, provide incentives for quality work, and transfer responsibility out of the regional shop.[17] The result was improved performance.

The management structures of the Maasai and Arusha projects also differed; the latter included a deputy project manager (or deputy team leader for the technical assistance team). This position had a positive effect on management behavior and on the control of assets. With a deputy, the project manager could focus on external relationships, allowing the deputy to spend full time on internal matters. IRD experiences in Indonesia, Jamaica, the Philippines, Tanzania, and Zaire all reinforce this observation. Effective internal administrative control is facilitated by freeing the project manager to focus on external coordination.

Supervision and Coordination

The projects reviewed here are relatively complex and management-intensive. That is, rather than being simple efforts to install certain technologies in rural settings, they involve the simultaneous introduction of a wide range of goods and services using untried mixes of technologies. The result is a demand for skilled management.

Managers must perform two functions well. First, they must delegate responsibility for performing a task and supervise the execution of that task. Second, they must coordinate the efforts of a varied cast of characters over whom they exercise little or no formal authority.

Successful supervision in IRD requires a clear work assignment, the specification of what is to be done while letting the subordinate determine how to do it, an opportunity for two-way communication during the assignment, and a recognition of successful performance. But the cases examined seldom exhibited these characteristics.

The most common situation was a reluctance to delegate responsibility. This reluctance not only characterized IRD projects, but it also permeated the administrative systems that surrounded the projects. Thus, the problem extended far beyond the nature of individual actors and could not be alleviated by simple solutions, such as changing managers or providing training in proper management techniques.

The problem's micro-level manifestations was a lack of delegated authority, whereas the macro version was an inability to decentralize decision making. Even when the rhetoric of decentralization was strong, the difficulty remained — politicians, civil servants, field workers, technical assistance personnel, and local-level leaders all were reluctant to see any control of resources slip through their fingers. The more unsure those on top felt, the greater their unwillingness to devolve authority and responsibility.

The paradox is that a prerequisite for a strong periphery is a strong and secure center. Bottom-up strategies should be preceded by top-down capacity building if they are to work in any but the most small-scale and low-priority projects.

Outsiders who write reports that call mainly for more coordination have usually failed to understand what is happening; nonetheless, IRD projects continue to devote an inordinate amount of time and energy to coordination.[18] In fact, a host of mechanisms have been developed to foster better cooperation and more synchronized delivery of services. Both formal and informal approaches have been used at interagency and beneficiary levels to overcome this hurdle. The approaches and lessons of experience are summarized in Table 3.

Although this table assembles experience about mechanisms that were used to help promote cooperation of implementing agencies and their coproduction of goods and services with beneficiary groups, the term "coordination" hides a wide variety of behaviors.

Sometimes it was merely information sharing—assessing the convergence or divergence of policies, providing price data, or letting a manager know about an occurrence that affected implementation. Other times it was joint action—fielding multiagency teams, changing priorities to fit with common objectives, or synchronizing the sequence of field activities. A third type of behavior was resource sharing—a line agency making training facilities available to a project, a project office making vehicles available to a local government unit, or a PVO lending some of its people to a local group to help complete a particular task.

The costs and benefits associated with these three dimensions of coordination are different, and the mechanisms to achieve them will vary both by dimension and by setting. Joint action is far more difficult to attain than resource sharing, which in turn is more elusive than information sharing. These distinctions, and the appropriateness of different actions, are often lost in discussions of (and calls for more) coordination. In fact, overuse of this word is itself a barrier to more effective implementation. The same weakness is characteristic of the term "financial management," which often emphasizes expenditure control without understanding other important dimensions of financial procedures.

Financial Procedures

IRD is seldom undertaken in locations where organizations have excessive resources. Typically, government bodies and beneficiary organizations lack financial resources. The lack of funds often produces situations in which new opportunities cannot be seized or activities begin at the wrong point in the agricultural cycle.

Coordination also is facilitated by a resource buffer. When project funds are not forthcoming, responsible project officers often cannot meet or tenders cannot be let because a warrant has not arrived. Implementation, therefore, suffers a setback. Inadequate service delivery and delayed construction often stem from short-term shortages in funds.

There are many reasons why this happens. Treasuries and central banks are notorious for releasing funds slowly, even when those funds come from a donor. The longer these resources can be used to generate income or to cover shortfalls elsewhere, the better for the financial institution (or, in some cases, a few individuals).

Even when funds have been released, control over them is often not devolved to the field level. Implementing ministries commonly keep control over funds in a national office and allow them to trickle out only in response to intense

TABLE 3

Mechanisms to Coordinate Service Delivery

FORMAL MECHANISMS	INTERAGENCY COORDINATION	AGENCY-BENEFICIARY COORDINATION	IRD EXPERIENCE
	• Interagency coordinating or advisory committees (standing) • Matrix organizational structures • Liaison office at port or central ministry • Interagency task force (temporary) • Binding cooperative agreements • Loaning of personnel between agencies • Cost sharing • Joint training and orientation courses for agency personnel • Copies of reports sent to heads of other agencies • Fixed reimbursement agreements • Single report format used by two or more cooperating agencies • Existence of an independent monitoring and evaluation entity • Merging of agencies • Creation of an incentive system (financial, promotional, professional) to encourage working on joint projects • Field teams are interagency staff	• Beneficiary participation in decision making and/or monitoring of the project • Formal staff participation in project-linked beneficiary organization meetings • Orientation courses for beneficiaries • Requiring contribution by beneficiaries to project costs (labor, money, materials, etc.) • Periodic public meetings of staff with the community • Use of paraprofessionals and local volunteers • Beneficiary inclusion in staff training workshops • Beneficiary membership on standing committees and task forces • Beneficiary representative at staff meetings • Policy of staff recruitment from local area — sex, ethnicity, and class also considered	For policy and objectives to be taken seriously by bureaucrats or beneficiaries, formal coordinating mechanisms must be established. Committees, liaison offices, task forces, joint training, and report sharing all work at the interagency level, but single report formats often create more conflict than coordination, and both formal incentive systems and matrix structures work better in theory than in practice. At the beneficiary level, participation in decision making through committee membership and input contribution are important. Inclusion in training workshops also helps. The record of improvement based on staff recruitment from the area is mixed, however. Coordination is more political than technical. Different local contexts will cause identical mechanisms to produce varied results.

TABLE 3 (Continued)

	INTERAGENCY COORDINATION	AGENCY-BENEFICIARY COORDINATION	IRD EXPERIENCE
INFORMAL MECHANISMS	• Lending of resources (personnel, transport, etc.) by one agency to another on an informal basis • Use of informal information systems by decision makers • Encouragement of informal communication between agency staff (through inter-agency sports competition, weekend staff retreats, occasional seminars, etc.) • Having participant agency offices in the same location • Periodic meetings of agency decision makers on an informal basis • Staff participation in agency decision making • Use of a supportive management style by supervisors • Use of a bargaining strategy with external actors, rather than reliance on preset rules	• Availability of staff in an office accessible to the beneficiaries (open on market days, for example) • Encouragement of agency personnel participation in beneficiary organizations (civic, social, religious, etc.) • Posting of project objectives, target dates, etc., where they can be viewed by beneficiaries • Conducting businesses and writing reports in the beneficiary dialect • Holding staff meetings at unofficial locations (church, home of farmer, school, etc.) • Making project facilities available for beneficiary meetings and building facilities with this in mind	Formal mechanisms will not produce results unless informal practices are supportive. All of these mechanisms help. Most important at the interagency level are resource sharing, informal communication and meetings, staff participation in decisions, supportive management style, and bargaining attitude. At the beneficiary level all are necessary and should be encouraged. Flexible project designs, delegated authority, and performance-oriented (rather than control-oriented) management are needed to facilitate informal dynamics. If evaluations are not sensitive to informal behavior they are likely to recommend inappropriate remedies for misdiagnosed problems.

pressure from project managers and their allies. These problems have been observed in all the country settings reviewed in this book.

What is less commonly appreciated, however, is that the way donors do business can add to the difficulty. For example, in the Bula-Minalabac project in the Philippines, construction, coordination, and ministry effectiveness were all undermined by the donor's reimbursement system. The project had been designed in discrete phases, with each phase targeting a geographic section of the project area. AID repayment was based on a practice called fixed amount reimbursement, that is, a fixed price was negotiated for the AID portion of each phase. After the construction of roads, buildings, and canals was completed, the facilities would be checked to ensure that they were built to the specified standards. The donor funds would then be released.

This practice was originated to finance the reconstruction of schoolhouses destroyed by typhoons. The practice worked well, but when it encountered the more complex world of IRD, it ran into trouble.

In the Bula-Minalabac project, the discrete phases envisioned in the design were abandoned. The effective management of crews and use of equipment dictated that sections of the later phases should be begun before the earlier ones were fully completed. However, since donor reimbursement was geared to finished phases, the lead line ministry, in this case the Ministry of Agrarian Reform, encountered acute cash-flow problems. The more management succeeded in reaching its goals, the more devastating the financial crisis became. The project's own funds ran out, but no AID funds were forthcoming. The result was paralysis and protest. Initial donor procedures had penalized good management.[19]

Similar problems have been documented elsewhere. For example, overburdened economies, such as Tanzania's, have been further strained by the need to provide front-end financing for project investments, with donors later reimbursing the government for the effort. This is, in effect, a loan from a poor economy to a wealthy donor.[20] The result is not devastating in terms of a single project, but the aggregate burden resulting from a proliferation of donor-assisted projects can overwhelm the abilities of developing countries with limited absorptive capacity.[21]

Financial management, then, is a key ingredient in managerial behavior. Unless financial procedures reflect the administrative and logistical complexity of IRD and the local situation, they may exacerbate problems of capacity and coordination.

Coordination requirements also apply to interactions between local people and outsiders, particularly technical assistance (TA) personnel. Since TA is a major element in most IRD efforts, the issues surrounding its application are discussed below.

Technical Assistance

TA plays an important role in the large-scale model of IRD and is also important in smaller efforts such as the CBIRD model in Indonesia.[22] Although an overemphasis on the role of outsiders gives an incomplete picture of the source of development initiatives, the management-intensive nature and the multi-sectoral focus of IRD combine to generate a great demand for scarce skills.[23] The result is a reliance on externally provided TA.

IRD experience suggests that two fundamental aspects of TA are important for service delivery and sustainability. The first, the contracting mode, affects the ability of TA to function. The second, the behaviorial mode, is important in determining whether there is a growing local ability to sustain IRD benefits. Both modes affect the type and value of services delivered and illustrate deficiencies common to the implementation of IRD programs in general.

Contracting Mode

IRD programs typically use large numbers of experts. Technicians with specific skills may either do short-term work or be assigned to long-term duty at a project site. Similarly, management specialists often carry out both short- and long-term assignments, but account for only a minor portion of the TA procured.

Technical expertise is acquired in four major ways. The first is through a personal services contract. This contract may make the expert a direct employee of the host government with operational responsibility, or it may place the individual in an advisory role with the donor responsible for the contract.

The second approach is to contract with a university to provide the required technical expertise. Whereas the first approach stresses the skills of an individual, this approach is based on the university's overall capability as an institution. The approach tends to be used when a major project component is research, such as crop variety trials, farming systems studies, or the establishment of a research center. A variant of this approach is when host country staff are trained abroad.

The third approach uses an organization to obtain individuals. A so-called "body shop" is hired to assemble a group of experts, get them to the project, and then provide them with logistical support. Although the people may be competent, they often have no long-term relationship to their employer. In this approach, the focus is on the individuals, but the contract is with the organization.

The fourth approach is to contract for a team. This requires a firm that specializes in development and has a relatively large cadre of permanent staff providing both logistical and professional support. The approach assumes that long-term career prospects and permanence in the organization provide incentives for quality work as well as ensure accountability. This approach has been called a management team strategy.[24]

Seldom do IRD projects use only one method to acquire technical assistance.

Instead, they often mix two or more contracting modes. In addition, direct-hire donor employees usually assist field efforts.

The record of success varies. Some types of long-term assignments are appropriate for the university contract, whereas others benefit from the management team approach. For example, the university is appropriate for research or teaching but has difficulty supporting ongoing action at the project level. The "body shop" consistently lags behind all the others in its ability to marshal and direct human resources in the field. The Maasai project in Tanzania provides an extreme example of a "body shop" approach where team leaders were unable to exert supervisory control over team members due to the transient association of both with the contracting firm.

The project's particular needs should be weighed and matched to the strengths and weaknesses of each option. However, a word must be inserted about the relationship between short- and long-term assignments.

Time Frame

Unfortunately, discussions concerning TA often deteriorate into debates about dichotomies: short/long, technical/managerial, and lots/little. But never are choices so simple.

Funds for TA are provided through the grant portion of most AID project budgets and by both grant and loan funds from the World Bank and some other donors. Host governments often do not give TA as high a priority as the foreign exchange component of a loan or the project's infrastructure dimension. Indeed, host governments commonly wish to keep to a minimum the long-term TA presence. As a result, short-term personnel are often preferred.

However, it is difficult to hold those who provide short-term assistance accountable for their recommendations. The depth of knowledge required to anticipate the impact of alternative courses of action is hard to obtain on a quick trip. Those who practice the short-assignment approach, however, can legitimately point out that long-term personnel often become so engrossed in details and so identified with the project that they lose their objectivity. Moreover, a long-term team has limited flexibility because the project is constrained by the skill mix incorporated into its original design.

Not surprisingly, the IRD experience indicates that a blending of both types of TA is most desirable. Each has strengths and weaknesses. The key to successful application of TA is managing the combination rather than selecting one over the other.

Effective management of TA requires more than just a contract-established method of accountability or an appreciation for the functions of both short- and long-term TA. Effective management also requires a vision of the appropriate role for TA to play. This involves dissection of the various modes of behavior that may be involved in its application.

Behavioral Mode

A key determinant of the effectiveness of TA personnel is the way they see and act out their roles.[25] If local capacity to perform functions temporarily handled by outsiders is not built, the contribution of TA to sustainability becomes questionable.

One approach to TA is to bring someone in to do the job. An engineer may be hired to oversee the construction of a road—that is, an outsider is engaged as a performer. This is the most common application of TA to IRD projects.

In the performer model, a temporary team or individual performs a specified set of technical activities and then leaves. The job may require a presence of one to five years, or only a few weeks or months. In either case, the emphasis is on a product resulting from the activity, and no attempt is made to build local skills. In an analytic exercise, the focus is on correct diagnosis and technically sound recommendations; in construction, it is on time, cost, and adherence to design specifications.

One advantage of the performer model is the outsider's freedom from local ties. When ethnic or age group connections place obligations on civil servants, they may find it difficult to resist pressure for preference in service delivery or diversion of resources. Outsiders do not suffer from this limitation.

The second approach to TA, the substitute model, is similar to that of the performer but focuses less on the product. This model is most common in the Arabian Gulf states, Papua New Guinea, and sub-Saharan Africa.

In this model, a qualified outsider fills a job until local talent is recruited and trained. The substitute model is often used when a local official is sent overseas for long-term training or, less frequently, when in-country institutions do the training. The model is also manifested by operational experts working in various countries. One problem is its tendency to support former colonial officials who may be short on technical skills.

In practice, outsiders find it difficult to separate the substitute from the performer role in a project demanding timely decisions and action. For this reason, an outsider directly attached to a project rarely becomes a true substitute or transfers his or her skills to a host country national.

Another approach to TA is called the adviser, although a more accurate description is that of teacher. This model reflects the view that development requires a substantial transfer of skills and technologies and that this transfer calls for a TA role that is filled by neither the performer nor the substitute.

In the teacher model, the outsider is placed in an advisory role rather than in a direct decision-making role. A key factor is the local counterpart who is expected to be the recipient of the advice. Success is defined as the transfer of skills to the counterpart, and thus a person focus replaces the product or job focus of the performer and substitute models.

This type of TA differs markedly from the performer approach. For example, an outsider may be engaged to conduct a cash-flow analysis of an irrigator association's operations. In the performer model, the report would be the main consideration. In the teacher model, a counterpart might be assigned for the duration of the study, and the ability of that person to prepare the report would be equally important. Moreover, the report would be seen differently. It would be expected to be written as a teaching device so that a reader also might learn how to conduct this type of study.

Although this model is commonly espoused in the IRD experience, it is less often practiced. In times of stress, long-term personnel slip quickly into the performer role. Short-term TA is usually based on the performer model, even when the long-term strategy emphasizes the teacher.

The fourth model of TA behavior has its roots in community development, organization development, and institution-building traditions. It is called a mobilizer.

Mobilizers combine advisory and advocacy functions. They help a community or organization increase its capacity to perform needed functions. Thus, coalition building, inspiration, skills development, and surrogate leadership are key activities.

Since this model emphasizes the ability of TA personnel to motivate others to act, priority is given to the establishment of processes that enhance local skills and encourage the institutionalization of local participation. Although this model shares characteristics with the teacher role, the mobilizer requires conflict management skills and the ability to analyze and articulate the process dimension of work.

Outsiders may be more effective mobilizers than nationals because the former usually have less to lose by helping to bring about change. An effective host country project manager may benefit from this phenomenon in the use of expatriate advisers.

Table 4 summarizes the characteristics of each of the four models and includes the IRD experience. Traditional TA relies on the performer model. Many projects in this study also use this model most extensively. Technicians are given specific problems to attack. This approach is to alleviate obstacles and polish the rough edges of a project design. In terms of purely technical issues, it makes sense. But IRD is management-intensive, and more attention must be given to interpersonal and organizational barriers to performance. One result is the need to consider alternative ways of applying TA.

The need for creativity in the use of TA also applies to local sources. For example, when technical failings were found in the infrastructure plan for the irrigation system of the Libmanan-Cabusao project in the Bicol region of the Philippines, the authorities removed the project from the regional National Irrigation Administration (NIA) office and placed it under a national NIA office of special projects, which was to redesign the system. This change was justified by the lack of redesign capability at the lower level.

TABLE 4

Behavioral Models of Technical Assistance

	Long-Term Implications	Short-Term Implications	IRD Experience
Performer	Production or service focus; temporary team or individual performs specified set of technically oriented activities; emphasis on completion (results); high priority on technical competence.	Product or service focus; team or individual performs specified set of discrete technical activities (e.g., management audit, agronomic analysis); emphasis on correct diagnosis and technically sound recommendations; low emphasis on work process; high priority on technical competence. Work may be done on single visit.	This is the most common style of TA. It is useful when specific, very technical tasks are needed, but it is inappropriate as a way to provide management assistance. Performers are free from kinship ties, and they are useful for implementing unpopular, but necessary, decisions. The overdependence on this style, however, blocks local capacity building and perpetuates dependence.
Substitute	Job focus; operational expert (OPEX) from outside does job, while local is overseas receiving training; high priority on work experience.	Not found.	This is a short-term solution that has achieved an almost permanent status in a few countries. It is as much an employment mechanism for colonials as a development device. It is better performed by volunteers, who are less jaded and more flexible, if less professional.
Teacher	Person focus; outsider seen in advisory, not decision-making role; accountable for transferring skills, knowledge to counterparts; priority given to appropriateness of process for transferring predetermined skills; high priority on academic training and technical skills.	Mixed focus—person and product; counterparts appointed for short termers; report seen both as substantive contribution and as teaching device to impart analytical skill; high priority on both writing and process skills; high priority on academic training. Work may be done on single visit.	Most long-term TA personnel claim to follow this model, but few do. When counterparts are transferred or unavailable, teachers become performers. Donor evaluations reinforce this drift by looking at TA "output." This approach is seldom used by short termers, but when performed well it can be effective on both a short- and a long-term basis. For this model to be adopted, it must be articulated and supported by the TA team leader or by the donor supervisor.

	Long-Term Implications	**Short-Term Implications**	**IRD Experience**
Mobilizer	Organizational focus; outsider seen in advisory and advocacy role; accountable for motivating others to act; priority given to process for enhancing local skills; coalition building and inspiration are critical activities; partnership with short-term TA is very important; high priority on personal commitment, compatibility, skills, and credentials that enable outsiders to deal with multiple organizational levels.	Mixed focus—product and organization; same as long-term focus but higher reliance on mobilizing actions and decisions in specific time frame; high priority on process skills for conflict management; writing skills and process analysis are also important; may not require report on each visit, however; good working relationship with both long-term TA and local groups critical for success. Work requires multiple visits.	This is a high-risk model—if it is performed poorly it can raise conflict without providing help. If local expectations are at odds with this role, little will be accomplished. When executed and received well, it is an effective approach to capacity building and management assistance. It is not easy to judge the effectiveness of TA people following this mode. However, any evaluations must be sensitized to it. It also requires local, team leader, and donor support.

Note: "Long term" refers to a continuous field presence of 12 months or more, while "short term" is anything less.

An alternative approach would have been to establish a temporary task force, composed of both national and regional staff, to do the redesign. This approach would have solved the problem while building local capacity. Thus, a teacher-performer approach might have been more effective than just a performer approach in facilitating sustainability.

Moreover, when sustainability is seen as a major objective, TA must be viewed in a different light—TA is not only essential for delivering goods and services to beneficiaries, but it is also a key element in building local capacities. The types of services needed from TA personnel may shift as greater recognition is given to preparing those who will inherit project functions. This emphasis may herald the rise of the teacher and mobilizer.

But choosing a preferred behavioral model is not adequate to improve TA impact. The organizational strategy must be supportive of the behavioral approach. Contradictions will arise when the TA and organizational strategies are at odds.

For example, implementation through a PMU is often combined with long-term TA cast in the teacher role. In this case, counterparts are recruited away from a permanent organization, placed in a temporary and vulnerable one, and then expected to digest knowledge from the TA experts. By the time this knowledge transfer has taken place, however, the PMU is planning to disband and the counterparts are set adrift. Thus, permanent institutions have been drained and local technicians or managers have been abandoned. A mismatch between organizational and TA strategies has led to limited capacity building. A combination of organizational bypass and individual focus inhibits sustained service delivery and limits the potential impact of a project. One way to lessen this problem is to strengthen the abilities of some local institutions to provide TA to others.

Local Technical Assistance

Contracting mechanisms, time frames, and behavioral models are not the only issues surrounding the use of TA. Another consideration involves the development of local sources to provide assistance to local clients.

The term "technical assistance" evokes an image of foreign experts dispensing advice or doing a job. Indeed, this is often the practice in IRD. But just as there are alternative behavioral models, so too are there alternative sources.

Upland Thai villagers, for example, hired a low-land rice farmer to come live among them and teach them advanced methods of rice cultivation.[26] Although the TA source was external to the village, it came from within the country.

Building a local center of excellence to provide assistance after donor resources are exhausted is a strategy for promoting sustained service delivery. When projects work through intermediary organizations, those organizations can become future sources of TA. In Botswana, for example, a few strong burial societies provided financial management skills and other assistance to other societies,[27] and in West Africa established credit societies have helped start new ones.[28]

The inability to focus attention and concentrate capacity provides a partial explanation for unsustained local organizations. The dispersion of effort and resulting inability to build viable beneficiary groups characterized IRDP II in Jamaica. If a few had gained the strength to assist others, the project might have had a longer-lasting impact.[29] Similar experience can be identified in Indonesia, Liberia, and Tanzania.

Strengthening local concentrations of teacher and mobilizer skills should be an objective for the application of imported TA. But a key question is where to build those skills and how to ensure that they will be used.

Client organizations may need process capacity to gain access to local skill strongholds.[30] That is, knowledge of how to contract for services and procedures for doing so may be lacking. Thus, both the suppliers and users of TA may need to be primed before the linkage occurs. Projects can be designed to perform this function, and the criteria for evaluating TA can be structured to take this situation into account.

Moreover, private and non-governmental organizations can be used. Often civil service restrictions are so great that the only way to obtain an adequate concentration of skilled people (and ensure that their skills will be applied) is to work outside government. In these situations, projects can be designed to act as matchmakers, bringing together local suppliers and users of organizational and technical services.

Adopting these approaches implies a radical departure from the common performer-oriented use of TA in IRD. It also has implications for appropriate approaches to management training institutions and training processes.

Training Practices

One important aspect of IRD implementation is training. Long-term degree training often takes place overseas, but immediate objectives are usually better served by staff training organized as a routine implementation activity. For example, LADD in Malawi has a training officer who oversees an extensive staff training program within the project area. Credit supervision, agricultural extension, and technical subjects typify the short courses.

Management training has also become an integral part of many IRD projects. Joint programming workshops are held repeatedly in Indonesia, the Philippines, and Tanzania. Retreats and staff brainstorming sessions are used in such countries as Jamaica and Liberia. These are especially common when provincial or regional capabilities are being strengthened, but they also take place within PMUs, PVOs, and lead line agencies.

There is, however, a remarkable pattern in the sources used to conduct on-site management training. Although local institutes of public administration (IPAs) could easily be tapped, this does not happen. Even when it was assumed

in the project design, such as in Liberia's Bong County project, little or no interaction takes place. Instead, TA funds are used to bring in outsiders or to pay
local experts who are not affiliated with IPAs. For example, Malawi's LADD
arranged for a course in supervision and management with the University of
Reading in the United Kingdom, rather than with the IPA at Mpembe.

The explanation is twofold—organizational and methodological. The organizational explanation emphasizes a lack of autonomy and a lackluster leadership
that characterize IPAs. Moreover, the upward mobility of civil servants is not
speeded by a teaching tour at an IPA. Instead, it can be a dead end. Budgets
are small, and influence is low. The result is an inward focus by institute staff
and a lack of interest by IRD staff about which skills an institute staff may possess.

The methodological explanation emphasizes the ineffective practices that
commonly characterize the training approach of IPAs. More specifically, IPA
training has six weaknesses:

- A place orientation—unrelated individuals are trained together because
  participant days and full use of the facility are deemed more important
  than improved job performance;
- A dictation orientation—participants are treated as recipients of faculty
  knowledge rather than as possessors of prior job-related knowledge;
- An inference orientation—hypothetical cases, rather than real issues and
  problems, are used to teach methods;
- A single-level focus—supervisors, middle managers, and senior staff are
  trained and treated separately;
- An overemphasis on organizational resources—a technique is equated with
  its use, and no attempt is made to assess organizational incentives or dis-
  incentives for adoption; and
- A discrete approach to training—training is treated as separable from the
  ongoing process of project management and therefore is undertaken in
  discrete units at distant places with trainees from unrelated fields.

These methodological weaknesses have reinforced the organizational problems
of many IPAs, especially in Africa, and have contributed to the poor linkage
between IPAs and IRD projects.

A more effective approach uses an action orientation with real work units.
Characteristics of this approach include:

- A link between training and work, using work groups as the basic unit
  of training;
- The use of real and current work-related problems of trainees as subjects
  material for workshops;
- The fostering of multilevel involvement in training to enhance supervisor-
  subordinate communication;
- The conduct of training at or near project sites when possible; and

- The use of an enhancement strategy that makes participant knowledge and skills the basis for training rather than relying solely on trainer expertise.[31]

This approach has registered success in such varied environments as Egypt, Indonesia, Kenya, the Philippines, and Tanzania. When local capacity to undertake this approach is built, it offers a way out of the technical assistance traps that threaten the sustainability of IRD.

Summary

The IRD experience suggests that organizational choices and management practices directly affect service delivery and offer explanations for observed differences in success. At the same time, no matter which organizational alternative is chosen, projects grow to reflect the class structure and organizational profile of the local environment. Although organization and management make a difference, the extent of that difference is bounded by local factors. Thus, there is no optimal way of organizing—there are tradeoffs, and the local situation determines the relative advantages of each option.

Nonetheless, some general lessons are clear. For services to be delivered, authority should be concentrated. Dispersed authority leads to breakdowns in coordination and performance.

In all settings, successful implementation is closely related to the ability of managers to recognize and use informal procedures, relationships, agreements, and communication channels. Informal processes are appropriate in all organizational models, but they require project designs that allow sufficient scope for innovation and flexibility. This, in turn, requires a real decentralization of authority to the field level.

Herein lies a dilemma. Concentrated authority is required for efficient delivery of goods and services, whereas delegated authority serves the broader implementation goals of rural development such as institutional development and the transfer of skills and technologies to the grassroots. Finding the appropriate balance in each particular setting is at the heart of the development management challenge.

A manager focusing on external coordination supported by a deputy focusing on internal supervision and control can help resolve the dilemma. In fact, this approach characterizes several well-run projects. TA teams also improve their performance when they adopt a similar arrangement.

Poorly conceived financial management procedures, approaches to TA, and types of training all impede IRD service delivery. But new, more promising approaches are emerging from the experience. They promise success not because they focus on service delivery alone, but because they look beyond administrative fixes to confront questions of sustainability and local action.

Notes

1. Charles F. Sweet and Peter F. Weisel, "Process versus Blueprint Models for Designing Rural Development Projects," in George Honadle and Rudi Klauss, eds., *International Development Administration: Implementation Analysis for Development Projects* (New York: Praeger, 1979), 127–145.

2. For discussions of dualism, see Roger Leys, ed., *Dualism and Rural Development in East Africa* (Copenhagen: Institute for Development Research, 1973). For the enclave approach, see the literature on institution building.

3. B. B. Schaffer, "The Deadlock in Development Administration," in Colin Leys, ed., *Politics and Change in Developing Countries* (Cambridge, England: Cambridge University Press, 1969), 177–212.

4. See, for example, Uma Lele, *The Design of Rural Development* (Baltimore, MD: Johns Hopkins University Press, 1975).

5. See *Organization for Agriculture-based Rural Development* (Washington, DC: Public Administration Service, 1975); and George Honadle, "Organization Design for Development Administration: A Liberian Case Study of Implementation Analysis for Project Benefit Distribution" (Ph.D. diss., Syracuse University, 1978).

6. Honadle, "Organization Design."

7. Jerry Silverman, Paul Crawford, and George Honadle, *AID Assistance to Local Government: Experience and Issues* (Washington, DC: Development Alternatives, Inc., 1982).

8. These findings are based on a review of the organizational literature conducted in 1980.

9. See Jerry VanSant, *Community Based Integrated Rural Development (CBIRD) in the Special Territory of Aceh, Indonesia*, IRD Field Report no. 4 (Washington, DC: Development Alternatives, Inc., 1979).

10. These categories represent a modification of elements common to successful private voluntary organization projects, as suggested in A. H. Barclay, Jr. et al., *Final Report: Development Impact of Private Voluntary Organizations: Kenya and Niger* (Washington, DC: Development Alternatives, Inc., February 1979).

11. David Korten, "Management for Social Development: Experience from the Field of Population" (Paper prepared for the conference on Public Management Education and Training, Bellagio, Italy, August 1976). It should be noted, however, that Korten's recommendation was based on observation of the successful program in Indonesia and did not anticipate the way that the matrix approach would be translated into project settings.

12. For the classic depiction of this, see Alvin W. Gouldner, *Patterns of Industrial Bureaucracy* (New York: The Free Press, 1954).

13. A similar conclusion emerges from a study of successful efforts in other Asian settings. See David Korten, "Community Organization and Rural Development: A Learning Process Approach," *Public Administration Review* 40, no. 5 (1980): 480–511.

14. Russel Stout, Jr., *Management or Control: The Organizational Challenge* (Bloomington, IN: Indiana University Press, 1980).

15. Thomas Armor, George Honadle, Craig Olson, and Peter Weisel, "Organizing and Supporting Integrated Rural Development Projects: A Twofold Approach to Administrative Development," *Journal of Administration Overseas* 18, no. 4 (1979): 276–286.

16. See Robert W. Clower, George Dalton, Mitchell Harwitz, and A. A. Walters, *Growth Without Development: An Economic Survey of Liberia* (Evanston, IL: Northwestern University Press, 1966); and David J. Gould, *Bureaucratic Corruption and Underdevelopment in the Third World: The Case of Zaire* (New York: Pergamon Press, 1980).

17. George Honadle and Richard McGarr, *Organizing and Managing Technical Assistance: Lessons from the Maasai Range Management Project*, IRD Field Report no. 2 (Washington, DC: Development Alternatives, Inc., 1979).

18. Robert Chambers noted that ignorance of how an organization works often hides behind calls for more coordination. See *Managing Rural Development* (Uppsala: Scandinavian Institute of African Studies, 1973), 25. For discussion of the information and resource components, see Rudi Klauss, "Interorganizational Relationships for Project Implementation," in G. Honadle and R. Klauss, eds., *International Development Administration: Implementation Analysis for Development Projects* (New York: Praeger, 1979), 146–167.

19. Jerry M. Silverman et al., *Bicol Integrated Area Development II (Bula-Minalabac Land Consolidation) Project Evaluation Report (Philippines)* (Washington, DC: Development Alternatives, Inc., 1981).

20. R. H. Green, D. G. Rwegasira, and B. Van Arkadie, *Economic Shocks and National Policy Making: Tanzania in the 1970s* (The Hague: Institute of Social Studies, 1980).

21. George Honadle and Jay Rosengard, "Putting 'Projectized' Development in Perspective," *Public Administration and Development* 4, no. 3 (1983): 299–305; and Elliot R. Morss, "Institutional Destruction Resulting From Donor and Project Proliferation in Sub-Saharan African Countries," *World Development* 12, no. 4 (1984): 465–470.

22. Donald R. Mickelwait, George Honadle, and A. H. Barclay, Jr., "Rethinking Technical Assistance: The Case for a Management Team Strategy," *Agriculture Administration* 13, no. 1 (1983): 11–22.

23. Judith Heyer, Pepe Roberts, and Gavin Williams, eds., *Rural Development in Tropical Africa* (New York: St. Martin's Press, 1981).

24. Mickelwait et al., "Rethinking Technical Assistance."

25. This section draws on George Honadle, David Gow, and Jerry Silverman, "Technical Assistance Alternatives for Rural Development: Beyond the Bypass Model," *Canadian Journal of Development Studies* 4, no. 2 (1983): 222–240. For related discussion, see Francis Lethem and Lauren Cooper, *Managing Project-related Technical Assistance: The Lessons of Success*, World Bank Staff Working Paper no. 586, 1983; and Irving J. Spitzberg, Jr., ed., *Exchange of Expertise: The Counterpart System in the New International Order* (Boulder, CO: Westview Press, 1978).

26. Peter Kunstadter, "Subsistence Agricultural Economics of Lua and Karen Hill Farmers, Mae Sariang District, Northwestern Thailand," in P. Kunstadter, E. C. Chapman, and S. Sabhasri, *Farmers in the Forest: Economic Development and Marginal Agriculture in Northern Thailand* (Honolulu: University Press of Hawaii for the East-West Center, 1978), 92.

27. Chris Brown, "Locally-initiated Voluntary Organization: The Burial Societies of Botswana," *Rural Development Participation Review* 3, no. 2 (1982): 11–15.

28. Kenneth Little, *West African Urbanization: A Study of Voluntary Associations in Social Change* (Cambridge, England: Cambridge University Press, 1965).

29. George Honadle, Thomas Armor, Jerry VanSant, and Paul Crawford, *Implementing Capacity-building in Jamaica: Field Experience in Human Resource Development*, IRD Field Report no. 9 (Washington, DC: Development Alternatives, Inc., 1980).

30. Jennifer Ann Bremer, "Building Institutional Capacity for Policy Analysis: An Alternative Approach to Sustainability," *Public Administration and Development* 4, no. 1 (1984): 1–13.

31. George Honadle and John P. Hannah, "Management Performance for Rural Development: Packaged Training or Capacity Building," *Public Administration and Development* 2, no. 4 (1982): 295–307.

CHAPTER THREE

Enhancing Local Action

The development landscape is littered with unused goods and services—empty clinics, wasted fertilizer, ignored extension advice, and countless other inappropriate or unsustained responses to project implementation. There are numerous reasons for this poor record. National policies that make sustained response unattractive to villagers, unacceptable social consequences of using project products, administrative barriers, and lack of basic resources needed to use services have all constrained effective local response.

At the same time, successful responses have occurred. Success may take several forms, but it invariably involves action by rural people to adopt new technologies and to commit resources to achieve development objectives.

Local action is an essential part of the development process precisely because development is a process and not some predefined end condition. Development involves changes, the most important of which is in the attitudes and actions of those people who become participants—individually or in groups—in the process itself. Through participation in their own development, people have the opportunity to strengthen their capabilities and build their own channels for expression and accountability.[1] In an ideal world, local action would be the beginning of a development effort rather than a response to an outside initiative. But even in an imperfect world, local action is the key to sustainability.

Types of effective action differ with particular development initiatives. The response needed for increasing agricultural productivity is distinct from that desired to implement a family planning program. With both economic and social development initiatives, however, some changes in behavior on the part of rural people will be required for success. In addition, development initiatives will not be sustained unless beneficiaries make some form of resource commitment to support those initiatives.

Unfortunately, changes in behavior and commitment of resources frequently do not take place. Furthermore, project histories indicate that problems of inadequate response are neither sector-specific nor area-specific. Instead, they permeate the entire development experience.

This experience base predates the initiation of the projects reviewed in this book. Indeed, most of those projects were designed to avoid nonresponse. Some succeeded, and others were notable failures. This chapter examines the different strategies these projects used to generate a sustained local response, and it assesses the relative merits of those strategies based on their record.

Since it is the intended beneficiaries who do or do not respond to project products, a focus on beneficiary perceptions and behavior might be expected to dominate attempts to forge this linkage. This, in fact, is the case. Four basic strategies are evident in the IRD experience:

- Conducting beneficiary-oriented studies;
- Establishing beneficiary-oriented organizations;
- Practicing beneficiary-oriented management; and
- Providing beneficiary-oriented incentives.

Sometimes these approaches are used together; in other cases, they are used individually. Some cases provide clear examples of how and why a strategy did or did not work. Others are far less clear in terms of results and possible explanations for them. This chapter examines the range of experience and attempts to extract some lessons from it.

Mapping the Local Landscape

Rural villagers do not initiate donor-supported rural development projects. Instead, these projects emerge from the professional interests, career prospects, and bureaucratic mandates of donor staff, combined with the political interests of donor and recipient organizations. In this world, one way to improve the quality of project designs and the probability that beneficiary response will be achieved is to increase civil servants' understanding of the perspectives, priorities, and behavior of villagers. This is the purpose of beneficiary-oriented studies. Some studies are intended to inform donor staff, whereas others are directed primarily at local civil servants and project personnel. Both are needed.

The development record suggests that donor ideas about projects are as likely to spring from individual obsessions and organizational fads as from any appreciation of conditions in specific localities.[2] Even local civil servants are often far removed in education, experience, and world view from their village clients. In fact, the requirements for bureaucratic membership and advancement usually widen the gap between civil servant and villager. At the same time, the myth is often maintained that civil servants who have village origins can speak for villagers. This is not often the case. Thus, the need to use studies of beneficiaries to inform project implementers and designers is a real one.

Although these studies may carry many labels, such as farming systems research, multipurpose surveys, or social soundness analyses, two basic types emerge from the experience: project focused and nonproject focused.

Project-focused Beneficiary Studies

When analysis of beneficiaries is geared to a particular project intervention, it may take place as part of the design process or during implementation. Theoretically, both approaches should help inform managers and policy makers of ways to improve projects to serve beneficiaries better. However, the record of turning new findings into improved processes is spotty.

Social soundness analyses, for example, are a standard component of project design documentation of the United States Agency for International Development (AID). But these analyses seldom identify real social constraints to beneficiary action. Instead, the tendency is to gloss over political and value problems, to stress idealized views of group solidarity, and to show how the project might reach some specified target group. A prime example is the social soundness analysis carried out for the Bula-Minalabac Integrated Area Development Project in the Philippines, but this case is not atypical.

Another example is the field study that preceded the design of the Maasai Range Management Project in Tanzania.[3] In this instance, the project proposed to bring about fundamental social changes, such as turning nomads into settled ranchers and altering the basis of the relationship between the Maasai and their cattle from social status, religion, and companionship to production for market sale. Although the difficulties were too obvious not to note, they were seriously underestimated.

In a few cases, studies bridged the gap between subproject design and project implementation. In the Save the Children's Community Based Integrated Rural Development (CBIRD) Project in Indonesia, reconnaissance methods were used to assess the needs and commitment of local villages to decide which localities would receive project assistance. This approach worked well, not because the studies were sophisticated but because the use of the data was followed by a participatory style of management and supported by the project's small-scale, focused nature.

Project-specific beneficiary studies often take place during implementation. For example, during implementation, temporary specialists and the project anthropologist conducted numerous studies of the effect of Tanzania's Maasai project on the Maasai. Unfortunately, the studies had no appreciable impact on either project redesign or staff behavior.

The provision of a specialist to perform a particular function may serve as a crutch for those who wish to avoid related tasks. Some technical assistance contract personnel assigned to long-term positions on the Maasai project viewed the anthropologist as a provider of socio-cultural services to the expatriate contract team. This removed much of the communication burden of the counterpart role from their shoulders. That is, the technicians could focus entirely on technical problems because the anthropologist would handle cultural and relationship issues. The result was lack of serious attention to beneficiary analyses. Other factors, such as the predominance of non-Maasai as project staff and a local perception of the project mission as reforming the cantankerous Maasai, exacerbated the situation.

Although the Maasai project is an extreme case of the poor use of beneficiary studies to improve service delivery, it is in fact consistent with practice elsewhere. For example, although a study of farm records in Jamaica generated interesting and potentially useful data, it had little impact on the Second Integrated Rural Development Project (IRDP II).

Thus, the record of project-level beneficiary studies contributing to modifications that enhance beneficiary response is poor. This is not necessarily a result of poor studies. It also stems from multiple factors blocking the use of study findings. Among those factors are the rigidity of project designs; lack of incentives for civil servants to respond to beneficiary needs; and the fact that these studies are usually afterthoughts, occupying a peripheral position in the implementation process.

Nonproject Beneficiary Studies

The second approach to beneficiary analysis involves studies to inform decision makers on a broader, nonproject basis. These studies may be academic, supporting a doctoral thesis, or they may be applied studies commissioned by donors to inform their organizations of local conditions. The academic model is widespread with anthropologists, agricultural economists, and farming systems specialists found throughout the developing world.

The applied model has multiple variations. Some studies may become so outsized that they assume the status of a project themselves. The Bicol Multipurpose Survey in the Philippines is an example of this phenomenon. Other cases include the numerous agricultural sector analyses conducted in West Africa.

The beneficiary study record becomes similar to that of project-level studies. In the Philippines, for example, an analysis of peasant perceptions was conducted in the Bicol region. The title of the report was "Let My People Lead," but the result reflected more curiosity about and lip service to participation than any attempt to let rural ideas actively guide project designs.[4] This study, commissioned in the early 1970s, identified improved housing as a top priority for villagers. Yet five years later, housing programs were still noticeably lacking from donor and local government portfolios in this area.

A recent initiative by the AID country mission in the Philippines represents an attempt to identify different household survival strategies throughout various areas of the country.[5] This approach has much to be said for it. But formidable political and procedural obstacles make it unlikely that the lessons of these assessments will be incorporated into programs that truly respond to villager needs. A similar attempt to identify the poorest of the population was undertaken in

Indonesia, and the results seem to be of similarly limited use.

Thus, neither micro nor macro beneficiary analysis has an encouraging record. Particular explanations vary by place, but one generalization consistently emerges from the experience: when learning is separated from action, the record does not improve.

A second explanation is related to the political nature of IRD. Frequently, political obstacles arise that prevent governments from adopting and implementing the requisite public policies needed to support appropriate development efforts. In other cases, difficulties lie, not with the intentions of governments, but with their inability to affect their programs in territories over which they exercise formal jurisdiction.[6] Sometimes, seeming political commitment to participatory local development may, in reality, be simply a recognition that rural mobilization can be an effective tool for increasing government control of the population. Civil servants learn quickly how to co-opt local initiative, controlling it rather than stimulating it.[7] In this environment, beneficiary analysis is likely to be ignored, unless it provides information that serves political agendas. But that kind of information may be sensitive. There are many reasons why learning is separated from action and why beneficiary analysis seldom improves the link between implementation and sustainability.[8] An approach that merges learning with action is the building of local organizations.

Building Local Organizations

A common project strategy to obtain response is to co-opt or create a beneficiary-oriented organization. This strategy emphasizes the action component of the learning/action dichotomy and is an extremely widespread practice in IRD. Local organizations can facilitate collective action by helping people make decisions or reach consensus and by providing a communication link with supervising agencies and project personnel. Often local organizations are valuable as channels of information about needs for specific services. Moreover, because they may be primary users of these services, local organizations have an important role in planning and implementing service delivery. And as vehicles for distributing benefits, they can support project equity objectives.

Examples of these local organizations abound. A typical model is represented by the cooperatives established by the Bong and Lofa County Integrated Agricultural Development projects in Liberia. Other examples include the irrigator associations and compact farms in the Bicol region of the Philippines; the development committees of IRDP II in Jamaica; and numerous cooperatives, ranchers' associations, fishermen's groups, and village organizations scattered throughout the IRD landscape. All of these organizations were expected to serve as communication channels during implementation and then to become the inheritors of project functions in the post-project period.

The purposes of a beneficiary organization are to enhance participation by providing beneficiaries a mechanism that they consider to be their own, and to support sustainability by creating a local entity that can continue appropriate project functions after the project ends. Generally, these local organizations are created as, or become satellites of the IRD project. A beneficiary organization is more likely to be a project creation than part of the local landscape before the project began. In any case, it is useful to review the implementation experience with these organizations and to draw characteristics of success from that experience.

Implementation Experience

Organizational placement strategy influences the types of problems that plague the introduction and development of beneficiary organizations. When a lead line agency that incorporates staff from multiple sectoral agencies is used, there is likely to be competition to determine which model the local organizations will follow. This competition occurs because line ministries usually have traditional relationships with certain local entities. For example, when the first IRD field project began implementation in the Bicol, the Ministry of Local Government and Community Development championed its group, the Samahang Nayon, as the basic unit in the irrigators' association. At the same time, the National Irrigation Administration favored its model, called a compact farm, and the Ministry of Agriculture used a different version of an organziation with the same name. The amount of time and energy that was spent debating the relative merits of each group during the first two years of implementation was phenomenal.

This problem is much less likely to occur when either a project management unit (PMU) or a subnational government unit implements a project. The PMU's autonomy allows the imposition of its own organization. Provincial or regional development efforts usually fund multiple subprojects that use different local organizations, thus satisfying several sectoral agencies. Experience in Indonesia, Liberia, Malawi, and Tanzania supports this observation.

IRD experience in Jamaica is similar, but presents a complicating factor — the question of whether to use a pre-existing organization at all. This issue can consume much attention since beneficiary groups are not monolithic, and different factions will want the project to link itself to the organization that favors them. The use of any local organization may be seen in political terms by local leaders. Party officials, landlords, merchants, and farmers will all have competing agendas.

Moreover, those decision makers' agendas may be incompatible with successful implementation of a local organizational strategy. When this is the case, two styles of derailment can occur: avoidance and sabotage.

The avoidance reaction is exemplified by a subproject component of the Provincial Area Development Program (PDP) in Indonesia. A calf-raising subproject on the island of Madura was being established. As discussions and analyses proceeded, it was realized that the scheme could generate significant income. As a result, civil servants became reluctant to use a beneficiary organization to implement the subproject. Instead of a local ranchers' association serving as the implementing agency, they wanted their own staff organization to take charge of the effort and reap its benefits.

In this case, a perception of tradeoffs between bureaucratic and beneficiary well-being complicated the implementation of a beneficiary organization strategy. This is a predictable phenomenon when expected benefit levels are high. If the subproject had been a small-scale, low-profile effort, it would have been less likely to evoke a predatory response.

Sabotage may result when a beneficiary organization is in place, but the project administration views it competitively. The idea of establishing a local organization and then devolving PMU functions to it is widespread. If a PMU builds capacity in a cooperative, the cooperative can take over marketing, credit, and input supply activities that the PMU began. But if PMU staff intend to perpetuate their positions, they may resist strengthening the cooperative. Instead, they are likely to seek training to build their own skills, and then use this to justify retaining key functions where the capacity lies—in the PMU itself. This happened in the Lofa County project in Liberia.[9] Thus, for project implementers to take beneficiary organizations seriously, there must be incentives for them to do so. This is true no matter which organizational placement strategy is used for the project.

In addition to bureaucratic perspectives, the village viewpoint is important, although usually underemphasized. In many locations, multiple projects compete for the time and attention of the same village leaders, model farmers, or even model beneficiaries. This is in addition to the normal social and work obligations that are often demanding in rural societies. Moveover, the rural social and agricultural calendars seldom coincide with the budgetary cycles and fiscal years of local governments or international donors. The result is a squeeze, with beneficiary organization leaders receiving pressure from above to use time a certain way and resistance from below. Thus, local organizations may be seen as a burden. African, Asian, and Latin American IRD experience all reflect this problem.

Just as a disparity often exists between project resources and rhetoric, so too local organizations are often expected to engage in functions that may be contradictory. Many of these units are actually established to funnel credit for input supplies to farmers and to provide peer pressure to improve the repayment record. Thus, these organizations begin life dependent on a project for resources, while saddled with the role of project policeman. To expect these organizations to evolve naturally into representatives of farmers with independent resource bases is unrealistic. Yet these expectations have been the norm in IRD experience.

The difficulty of advancing from what is to what is intended is demonstrated by the attempt to mold IRDP II development committees in Jamaica. In this case, the project-linked committees had great difficulty evolving away from their parasitic reliance on the project.[10]

Overall, the record of using a beneficiary organization strategy to enhance beneficiary response and improve chances for sustainability is mixed. At the same time, enough successful cases have emerged to suggest some of the characteristics that are needed to make the approach work.

Successful Strategies

Local organizations range from functional groups such as small farmer marketing cooperatives to social or religious bodies with no apparent development role.[11] Most communities have an official or semi-official development committee, such as the Indonesian Lembaga Sosial Desa, with close links to formal local leadership. These groups vary in terms of how representative they are of the community and their state of vitality, but even a moribund group can become a development resource.

Successful local organizations can play positive roles as vehicles for:

- Providing two-way flows of technical information that support those individuals who try new approaches and break down barriers between groups or individuals;
- Reducing risk to a minimum and practicing economies of scale;
- Adapting project activities to local conditions;
- Marshaling local resources;
- Achieving greater political and economic independence for local people by exercising influence over locally based administrative personnel and asserting claims on government; and
- Coordinating and spreading the benefits of outside assistance.

In many rural societies, specific groupings may emerge for specific functions: maintenance and repair of irrigation systems, construction of a school, or installation of a portable water system. Often the most successful organizations are those of this type, beginning with a single function that satisfies some immediate local concern. Yet these temporary groups often become permanent. Or they may move on to other activities, despite failing to achieve the initial goal or while waiting to do so.[12]

Historically, most local organizations have not been based on broad, participatory decision making. Or if oriented toward the poor, they have often lacked the resources and higher level support necessary to be effective. Successful organizations, in contrast, gain legitimacy with the poorer elements in the community by addressing their specific needs, building trust, and achieving widespread user satisfaction. The process of developing these organizations requires management ingenuity, particularly in areas lacking social cohesion and traditions of broad-based decision making. It also requires considerable time.

Even so, new problems may arise. Majority rule may still lead to majority discrimination against the very poor, who are the stated target of most IRD projects.[13] Special attention may be required to prepare the most marginal members of the community for genuine participation. One approach, used successfully by the CBIRD project in Indonesia, is a variant of the single function concept. The project gave the poor the opportunity to participate initially in small functional working groups so that they could gain the experience and skills to prepare them for participation in broader community organizations. Through interaction in the working groups and community organizations, the poor had opportunity to gain acceptance and recognition by members of the larger, more established groups.

Similarly, in several Latin American countries, communities have formed civil improvement associations to plan and implement specific rural works projects. An individual community commits its own resources to these projects and petitions the government or other funding agencies for additional funds. Once a specific project is completed, these organizations may lie dormant until they act on the next felt need. But the organizations represent a resource that can be mobilized quickly in response to future needs.

One recommendation emerging from studies of local organization is that project designers should not propose a single organizational model—in terms of size, responsibilities, or structure—for a whole project area.[14] Instead, they should consider various alternatives. This was done in the Mandara Area Development Project in south Cameroon. The design team suggested that three alternatives were available. The project could:

- Ignore existing organizations and attempt to create new, multi-functional, development-oriented organizations at the village level or higher;
- Use existing single-function village organizations and attempt to increase their technical capabilities in the project activities with which they are involved; or
- Use an existing single-function organization and encourage its gradual expansion into more varied functions by increasing its participation in several project activities.

The first alternative—creating new organizations—was regarded as the most difficult since it required a political sponsorship that was not readily apparent. Village development committees, found elsewhere in Cameroon, were absent in the proposed area. This was the case because administrative authorities in the north, belonging to a politically dominant but numerically small ethnic group, suspected a potential political orientation in such groups dealings with development issues.

The second alternative—using existing organizations and increasing their capabilities—was regarded as the easiest since it most closely conformed to the present governmental vision of the objectives of rural development projects in Cameroon. The third option lay between the first two. By gradually encouraging the formation of a modest community body capable of dealing with several development needs and organizing a common response to them, project implementa-

ters would be less likely to threaten an administration concerned about excessive decentralization.[15]

Thus, the IRD experience supports particular sides on the issues of how many functions to begin with and whether to use a single model. Another recurring issue involves the boundary of local organizations. The spatial arrangement of an irrigation area may crosscut administrative boundaries such as municipalities or provinces. The record in this project sample is not clear. Land development in Jamaica, for example, followed watershed boundaries and encountered trouble by bifurcating communities. Irrigation organizations in the Philippines had similar problems, but they stayed with the resource-based boundary and overcame the difficulties.

Even when a project using a topographical boundary for satellite organizations encountered failure, the choice of boundary did not seem to be the major determining factor. Because a single-function beginning and a resource to manage appear to be related to success, it would usually be preferable to build on the boundaries of the resource base rather than on political boundaries that reflect historical circumstances more than future potentials. Nevertheless, much energy may be required to deal with boundary-related conflicts. The inheritance passed from a project to local organizations is seldom purely positive.

Viable local organizations are a necessary, although not in themselves sufficient, condition for successful IRD. Without the support of local organizations, the best technical packages and the most skilled administrative personnel are not likely to elicit effective responses from the rural poor. Although beneficiary-run organizations are no panacea for local problems, at certain times and places they may represent critical vehicles for providing the link between project-related services and village use.

Beneficiary organizations that contribute to rural development tend to possess attributes that are discussed throughout this book. A summary of key characteristics is displayed in Table 5 along with some lessons from the IRD experience.

Supporting Participatory Approaches

The discussion of beneficiary studies and organizations identified a common weakness in the link between formal adoption of these strategies and actual bureaucratic behavior. Without an incentive structure that rewards the use of beneficiary analysis or the strengthening of local organizations, implementers are apt to follow a course of action that relegates beneficiary perspectives and initiatives to a secondary priority. This situation points to the need for the third way to support positive response among beneficiaries—the practice of beneficiary-oriented management.

Two aspects of beneficiary-oriented management are particularly important. The first is participatory management; the second is bureaucratic reorientation. These issues are discussed below after a review of common constraints to effective beneficiary-oriented management.

TABLE 5

Beneficiary Organization Characteristics

Dimension	Desired Characteristics	IRD Experience
Resource Base	• Should control a renewable natural resource • Should establish and control its own budget • Should learn to generate new resources • Should be a resource base that can be managed better with collective action	A monopoly over a natural resource, such as irrigation water or woodlots, is a key to sustainability. Project financing or access to credit will evoke a response, but it may be short lived. Training and technical assistance in the exploitation of the resource base will be needed. The capacity to generate, budget, and manage resources may need to be built by the project. A vital resource base enhances chances for success, but a very large and visible one may attract predators.
Scale	• Should be matched to resource base • Should begin smaller rather than larger	If it begins too small and does not include key personalities, success may be doomed. If it begins too large, the effort may be so unfocused that leadership skills may not be built. Village boundaries, settlement patterns, and other pre-existing boundaries must be taken into account.
Operating Style	• Should be open and visible • Should be compatible with and use local informal management mechanisms • Leaders should be accountable to a broad constituency	An open operating style draws members and ensures that organizational benefits are distributed equitably. Training may be necessary to support such a style as well as accountability to a broad membership. Even training in elementary operations, such as running meetings, may be needed. Although common wisdom suggests that this will be rejected in many cultures, the IRD experience is that it is widely acceptable.
Membership	• Should be broad based • Should not exclude local elites • Should share a common interest in the management of the resource base	Although members must have a common interest—e.g., water—membership should not be limited to a narrow group. The ideal is to be "inclusive" rather than "exclusive," but organizational benefits must be distributed equitably.
Functions Performed	• Should begin as single function organization • Should be able to adapt to new or multiple functions through time.	The easiest way to cripple an organization is to force it to perform many functions before it can perform one well. Should begin with a single function—water management or marketing, for example—and learn to be effective before expanding its functions. This also gives it a clear place in the local organizational environment.

Dimension	Desired Characteristics	IRD Experience
Establishment History	• Should *not* begin as a mechanism for the project to control beneficiaries • Should build on local pride, self-perception, and sense of self-reliance • Should *not* be imposed by outsiders	If an organization is identified by locals as a means for outside elites to penetrate the locality and control their activities, response will be avoidance rather than involvement. In an area with a history of self-reliance, local pride can be harnessed to provide a participatory momentum. Consistency with traditional community norms speeds acceptance.
Linkages to Other Organizations	• Should develop informally • Should *not* be forced	Effective local organizations develop linkages with others and use multiple channels to influence their environments. If one organization is a captive of another, it is not apt to satisfy member needs. Vertical linkages can improve access to support and resources. Horizontal linkages can reinforce the application of technical and administrative skills within the community. A strategy of building the capacities of selected organizations to serve other organizations allows efforts to be focused and improves changes for sustainable success.

Management Constraints

Management or administrative constraints may work against the effective involvement of local people in development activities even when beneficiary participation is a proclaimed goal of these activities. Two categories of constraints are of particular importance – institutional factors and inappropriate design. These factors are interrelated. Variations in institutional capacity can thwart attempts to replicate even successful pilot projects. A design appropriate in one context may not work elsewhere, even if the technical package is sound.

Major institutional factors include:

- Administrative capacity;
- Access to resources by local institutions that are accountable to the poor; and
- Bureaucratic responsiveness to the needs and interests of the local poor.

One example of the importance of administrative capacity for local response was provided by PDP in Indonesia. Credit was a common element in PDP-funded subprojects. In the provinces of Central and East Java, where existing administrative structures for credit were relatively strong, the PDP strategy of extending credit to small local traders had a beneficial impact. Interestingly, different existing credit systems were used in the two provinces, based on preliminary assessments of institutional strength. But in each case, credit facilities were made more accessible, the process of loan application was simplified, and supervision of outstanding loans was strengthened.

Credit was also a major component of the PDP strategy in Bengkulu. In this case, however, virtually no credit infrastructure existed before PDP and the new systems did not take hold. As a result, credit delays had a serious impact on the plans of technical agencies responsible for individual subprojects. The heavy concentration of credit programs in the Begkulu PDP may thus be seen as an unnecessarily high-risk approach in which the attempt was made to institute a program requiring a relatively sophisticated and mature organizational base before that base existed.

Frequently, IRD projects depended on central governments for critical resources. This lack of local control over resources often introduced a major constraint to participatory objectives. For example, the Government of Zaire's difficulties in meeting budget commitments became a major problem for the North Shaba Rural Development Project. Funding cuts in late 1979 led to layoffs of 600 people, or two-thirds of the project's work force. Most of them came from the infrastructure subsystem, which ground to a halt. The lack of funds meant that the project staff had greatly reduced means of transport and were not reimbursed for travel expense. As a result, they were not able to maintain effective contact with farmers.[16]

These examples are typical of centrally designed programs that often do not adapt well to local institutional realities or differences in institutional environ-ments. The consequences are a dulling of incentives for local involvement and a further movement of control over decisions and resources toward central authority.

Government bureaucracies are poorly attuned to the needs and aspirations of the poor, principally because most development agencies came into being before participation became part of the dominant development paradigm. These agencies were designed for more centralized, service-oriented programs, and their bureaucratic structures, systems, and norms pose important barriers to effective local action.[17] Furthermore, as weak, newly independent central governments attempted to engage in nation building and bring their peripheries under control, bureaucratic practices became even more rigid.

Yet the activities of the poor in government programs are crucially affected by the ways those services are run.[18] For example, nearly all extension services are government run and function according to standard procedures, rules, and precedents. These often engender both inflexibility and slow response to field needs. Prospects and incentives, particularly for those working in the field, are typically unpromising. Often pleasing immediate superiors becomes more important than responding to clients.

Bureaucracies often claim to be the only competent overseer of the projects they plan and implement. This claim often begins with the donor agencies them-selves and it nourishes the syndromes of overbearing government and popular apathy that mark poverty in developing countries.[19]

Numerous development initiatives fail to generate appropriate local response simply because they do not make sense. In fact, what are diagnosed as manage-ment problems often result from ambiguous or unrealistic project designs.

Design deficiencies occur for many reasons. Frequently, there is pressure to implement projects quickly for political reasons or because of short budget cycles. Design work and even feasibility studies are often performed within boundaries defined by earlier decisions to proceed in any case. With their field of inquiry limited, designers often fail to observe potential constraints to local response in the project environment. This problem may be compounded by the common preference for the use of technical specialists whose very use for the design studies implies a preselection of relevant solutions. Although this selection may serve the application of expertise to anticipated project issues, it may also widen gaps in understanding of external, unanticipated realities. Moreover, data generated from these technically oriented design studies are often in a form that is of little use for planning feasible implementation strategies at the grassroots.

In IRDP II in Jamaica, for example, designers chose to repeat a development strategy that had been tried twice before in the area without notable success. The concept of paying subsidies to farmers for their participation in soil conservation schemes had been the basis of earlier programs that failed to ensure continued maintenance by farmers of the subsidized soil conservation works.

It did little to increase production or income on the hill farms. The experience of the earlier soil conservation programs evidently was ignored in designing IRDP II, which experienced parallel failings. Although the design flaws were well recognized by Jamaican project managers, they were reluctant to pressure AID to change a clearly inappropriate strategy for fear of alienating its support for this external resource-dependent project. AID, for its part, was reluctant to pull back from a project with recognized problems because of the existing political imperative to move money in Jamaica.[20]

Two design problems of particular importance to local action are the failure to consider adequately local perceptions of risk, and excessive project complexity. In general, designers should assume that proposed innovations will not earn a ready response from local people unless certain conditions exist. For example, innovation is more likely to be accepted in rural areas in which:

- People have been previously exposed to, and have accepted, other innovations;
- At least some portion of the community is highly motivated or open to change; and
- Traditional attitudes, institutional structures, and customs do not impose overwhelming social costs on early adoption.

When factors such as these do not support risk taking, project designs should schedule sufficient time and appropriate activities to build local interest and confidence. Most likely, this objective may be accomplished by building on co-operative solutions to specific farmers' problems. In many situations, actors commit themselves to a specific technical innovation without realizing the extent to which this behavior slowly and subtly, but irresistibly, induces additional changes in behavior.[21] But this may be a relatively lengthy process, and few project designs reflect the necessary patience.

Projects requiring a complex mix of planning, administrative, logistical, technical, and funding resources often result in local dependence and the yielding of control to outside elements. Moreover, upfront provision of outside services tends to constrain the commitment of local resources by project beneficiaries. Nevertheless, complexity is a common characteristic of IRD efforts from design to evaluation.

Complexity constrains local response from the perspective of donors as well as beneficiaries. If a project is highly complex, it is less likely that donor agencies or host agencies will encourage beneficiaries to become actively involved.[22] However, if a local population does not perceive that it has some control of, or influence over, project resources, a sustained positive response is unlikely.

For designers, there are difficult tradeoffs implied in these considerations. A widespread network of small projects may facilitate response but requires field staff and local linkages to a degree that is uncommon for either central governments or donor agencies. Spreading resources thinly over a large area may create serious difficulties for logistical and financial control. In fact, few examples exist of genuinely decentralized projects taking on complex, integrated tasks.

Historically, these tradeoffs have been weighted in favor of a large-scale approach. The emphasis continues to be on elaborate, administratively complex, and capital-intensive projects that rely heavily on imported technology and are suitable for cost-benefit analysis.[23] These projects tend to follow rigid designs, impose unmanageable recurring cost obligations, and be intrinsically anti-participatory from the outset.

The alternative to complexity is a sequential approach that begins with such elements as local irrigation schemes, provision of focused credit, or training programs that permit meaningful local involvement. However, these projects may be relatively administration- rather than capital-intensive; difficult to monitor and inspect because of geographic dispersion; unsuitable for complex techniques of project approval; and slow to implement, unless "they originate in popular enthusiasm."[24]

Participatory Management

Thus, a major implication of this discussion is that a sensitive awareness of local conditions, practices, and needs, combined with knowledge of the policy environment, is essential for development planning and management. Indigenous social and economic arrangements survive because they perform necessary traditional functions, are adapted over time to cultural peculiarities, and satisfy local needs. An understanding of the constraints and risks perceived by farmers is therefore part of the process of eliciting their perceptions of local needs and providing them with opportunities to participate in the process of addressing those needs.

One study has suggested three categories of essential local data requirements in projects targeted at small farmers. Similar requirements would apply to management of projects for other groups as well. These categories are:

- Data to understand and overcome the constraints on farmers imposed by environmental factors;
- Data to ensure that project components are adequate or to determine alternative ways of providing the needed services and knowledge; and
- Data to determine project focus and organizational capabilities within an area so that farmers receive the benefits of project activities.[25]

Project managers and staff always work in a state of imperfect knowledge when addressing constraints to local action. In addition, they may be faced with self-imposed limitations. For example, they may wish to avoid being accused of political meddling or may feel locked into rigid project blueprints or comfortable addressing only technical questions. To modify these perceptions and achieve more effective action on constraints, managers and staff need better information from designers and a wider range of management and organizational tools.

Much has been written about the value of villager-held knowledge, and it has become common wisdom that villager participation in project deliberations can lead to more effective local action toward development goals.[26] It has also been suggested that when civil servants and project staff experience a participatory management setting they will be more willing to involve villagers in project decisions.[27]

This is confirmed by experience with PDP subprojects in Indonesia. Two different districts in the Kalimantan Province had motorized fishing activities that the project supported. In both cases, the project supplied boats, motors, and nets. However, villagers in one location received two types of nets whereas in the other they received three. The difference is important because fishing is poor during three months of the year, except for the availability of a particular species of large fish. Whereas the two types of nets were appropriate for small fish and shrimp, only the third net was effective for catching the large fish.

In the district in which three nets were provided, villagers had been consulted during the design of the subproject. In the other case, they were not. The explanation for a participatory approach in one district but not in the other lies in the operational styles of the two district commissioners ("bupati"). One stressed a collegial style in his relationships with local line-agency personnel. He called it collective responsibility. However, the second followed an authoritarian approach. The subproject with only two nets was in the district of the authoritarian bupati, and the sectoral agency staff in that area were less interested in promoting villager participation in development decisions.[28] This case is especially intriguing because it strongly indicates that the determining factor was management style — all other factors were equal.

Another example of beneficiary-oriented management also comes from Indonesia. The CBIRD project in Aceh, implemented by the Save the Children Federation (SCF), practiced open management. This approach was applied at the level of both the SCF field office and village and subdistrict committees associated with the project.

At the field office, the application of open managment was largely a reflection of the style of the SCF Indonesia expatriate director. At his initiative, an air of easy informality permeated the SCF office, which was the base for more than 15 employees. Because of continuous movement between Aceh and the field, the number of persons working in the office at any given time was about one-half of the total. The fact that the SCF office and the residence of the director were in the same house contributed to the open atmosphere.

More important, there was a structured attempt to increase communication to a maximum degree. Staff meetings were held frequently, and staff problems or complaints were openly discussed. Reports, memoranda, and correspondence, except strictly personal material, were posted. This approach contributed to a well-informed and well-motivated staff.

Open management had its greatest impact at the village level. The introduction of this management style was a major innovation for an Indonesian village. The decision to adopt this style was made by the local committees themselves, but was largely influenced by the training that members had received under the auspices of SCF. Open management meant, in effect, that all expenditures, income, receipts, and accounts were routinely published and posted. The idea was accepted that the local committees were not closed groups but acted on behalf of the whole community. Therefore, the community had a right to know what was taking place. Committee meetings were open. Villagers participated in meetings, aided by training that enabled them to understand the proceedings and records of the committees.

A major result of this openness was the willingness of the community to isolate and remove corrupt leaders. The availability of information clearly showed that people were being victimized by some of their leaders and representatives. The result was that leaders were held responsible for their behavior in ways that had not been possible before. Another effect was a slight, but important, shift of power to the socially and economically disadvantaged.[29]

Although both these examples come from Indonesia, attempts by individual project managers to promote participatory management are common in the IRD experience. Botswana, Ecuador, Jamaica, Liberia, Niger, the Philippines, and Tanzania all provide cases in which the approach was tried and seems to have worked. A participatory work environment does help encourage organizational staff to share resources and authority with clients and to develop a service delivery style that emphasizes participation and cooperation. This work environment is characterized by shared decision making and problem solving, use of teams to set targets and monitor the performance of tasks, shared job-related information, and a nonauthoritarian organizational structure.[30] The approach assumes that people possess the capacity for responsible, self-directed, and self-controlled behavior. It also suggests that staff feelings of self-worth contribute to effective job performance.

Participatory management emphasizes a particular approach to leadership and supervision. The underlying theme is that a participatory style supported by a beneficiary-oriented policy can be a major stimulus for treating clients as colleagues and jointly improving the implementation process. Thus, the role of personal leadership is stressed. The issue's importance derives from the crucial role of agency or project staff as contact agents between local people and civil servants. Yet staff commonly control few resources and are ill prepared and poorly motivated.

A participatory management approach may take place independent of organizational placement—PMUs and private voluntary organizations are as suitable as permanent institutions for experimentation with participatory management. But the transience of personnel limits the ability to sustain this approach within temporary settings. Therefore, it is necessary to go beyond individuals and their ability to shape a work environment. The need is for a long-run refocus of bureaucratic procedures.

Bureaucratic Reorientation

"Bureaucratic reorientation" (BRO) is a new term to describe an old phenomenon—the attempt to make large impersonal organizations responsive to the people they ostensibly serve.[31] Others have documented activities of this nature in such places as Sri Lanka and the Philippines.[32] The IRD projects on which this book is based amplify the lessons of experience.

Among these projects, various types of BRO were attempted. For example, the design of new organizations and interagency relationships characterized work in Nepal and Ecuador. In the Philippines, the use of process documenters was a significant feature of the Buhi-Lalo Integrated Area Development Project. CBIRD's introduction of a beneficiary-inclusive information system in a field situation also represents an attempt at BRO.

BRO rests on three pillars in its attempt to construct humane and responsive organizations. The first is the personal style and leadership characteristic of participatory management. The second is the information function stressed by beneficiary-oriented studies. The third is a concern for structural factors affecting human relationships.[33]

Although BRO is not a widely followed approach on the empirical IRD landscape, a few projects focusing on subnational government entities such as Arusha Planning and Village Development Project in Tanzania and PDP in Indonesia stressed a combination of organizational learning and reorientation. Nonetheless, BRO required a scrutinizing of bureaucratic systems that seldom took place in IRD. It was more common to find problem definitions surrounding cattle (the Maasai project in Tanzania) or terraces (IRDP II in Jamaica) or irrigation water (most of the Bicol region projects in the Philippines) than it was to encounter IRD undertakings that viewed the bureaucracy as an important part of the problem and were designed to address this issue. Instead, when the problem was perceived, the IRD response was likely to be to try to bypass the issue entirely, such as in the Lofa and Bong County projects in Liberia. The tendency was to aim at easy, discrete, physical targets rather than at more elusive targets such as rural institutions and institutional networks.

When bureaucratic reorientation was attempted, information flow was usually seen as an important first step. In Nepal, the design of the Rural Area Development/Rapti Zone Project was predicated on a perceived need for decision makers to be more aware of village perspectives.[34] In Tanzania, the Arusha project used the methods of Paulo Freire to engage in dialogue with villagers and to incorporate their knowledge and values into a regional planning exercise.[35] The project even used aerial photography to show them their land from a different angle and to involve them in discussions of resource issues.

In PDP in Indonesia, a first step was to articulate what was meant by the program's institution-building objective and to examine which bureaucratic practices were obstacles to achieving it. A result was the identification of administrative procedures that rewarded nonperformance and poor relationships with beneficiaries. In the Aceh Province, responsibility for each project vehicle was assigned to one individual. That person received a standard monthly cash allotment to cover all fuel and routine maintenance costs. Any costs exceeding the allotment had to come from the individual's own pocket. If the total was not used, the civil servant could keep the amount that remained. Although this practice did reduce false and inflated expense claims, it also provided a strong incentive not to make frequent trips to isolated rural areas since these trips would increase fuel costs and the likelihood of minor repairs. Thus, the procedure deterred even dedicated and willing individuals from working collaboratively with villagers.[36]

When the impact of this procedure was identified, it was employed as a wedge to begin exploring structural obstacles to bottom-up development. The procedure was quickly grasped by provincial civil servants to show that it was not their poor intentions or irrationality that inhibited progress. This depersonalized highly volatile issues and made possible a step toward organizational self-criticism and learning.

In PDP, a dual set of objectives—beneficiary income production and institution building by government at the provincial level—signified the interrelationship between local capacity and rural well-being. This interrelationship is represented in Figure 2. At the same time, subproject activities were to be used as learning laboratories to build bureaucratic abilities to help villagers increase their productivity and income.

Figure 2 suggests the complexity of PDP's dual focus. The more concrete and romantic subproject emphasis on production can easily dominate institutional objectives. Moreover, intergovernmental relations introduced a factor that supported this proclivity—donor reimbursement procedures were designed to support only successful subprojects as measured by budget expenditure and production criteria of a traditional nature. The result was an inconsistency between targeted staff behavior and the incentives to support behavior. As a result, organizational learning was stifled and local distrust of decentralization was reinforced. It also became apparent that reorientation is needed in donor bureaucracies just as much as it is needed elsewhere.

In PDP, implementation decisions, not design configuration, posed this threat to sustainability. The project did have the latitude to emphasize organizational learning rather than subproject production, but risk-avoiding behavior by donor field staff followed the path most common in IRD—rhetoric for capacity building and resources for physical production.

This issue constantly appears on the IRD landscape. Performer-style technical assistance, reimbursement procedures geared to control of physical products, and evaluations centered on the achievement of financial disbursement and physical production targets all combine to focus the attention of management

FIGURE 2

DUAL FOCUS OF THE PROVINCIAL AREA DEVELOPMENT PROGRAM

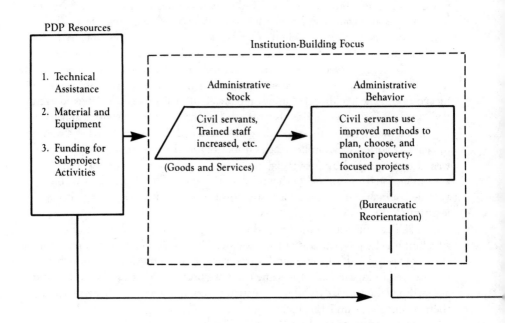

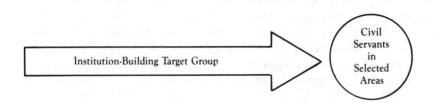

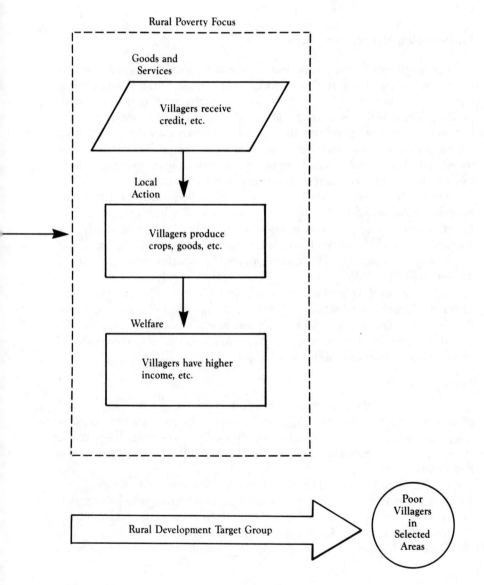

away from local initiative and learning and toward the accomplishment of pre-set production schedules by project staff.

Thus, the IRD experience with bureaucratic reorientation argues that, although management behavior and two-way information flows are important, structure is paramount. Political, bureaucratic, cultural, and even donor incentives must support the use of resources to achieve development and social-learning objectives. Otherwise, the installation of physical facilities will reign supreme, and local action will be treated as a secondary component of the implementation process.

Encouraging Beneficiary Action

The fourth major way to enhance prospects for local action is to provide some form of incentive to facilitate beneficiary response. This may be based on a policy decision at the national level, such as government marketing boards paying a higher price for a commodity produced in a project area, or it may be based on the assumption that the project technology addresses a basic need among the beneficiaries and itself is an adequate stimulus to encourage them to respond. Alternatively, project components may be designed to provide incentives for people to adopt new methods and behavior patterns.

These different approaches are not always mutually exclusive. For example, providing subsidized fertilizer, seeds, or equipment may be a project element but may also require prior concurrence among policy makers. Similarly, the attempt to increase security of land tenure may be a necessary initiative in a smallholder scheme, but it requires supportive policies or it cannot be implemented.

Policy issues will be explored more fully in Chapter 4. They are important in determining the sustainability of behavior changes, and thus they belong in the discussion of sustaining well-being. To conclude the examination of strategies for enhancing beneficiary response, however, two dimensions of incentives should be noted—meeting needs and sharing risk.

Meeting Needs

Most project designers assume that opportunity for increased income will provide enough incentive for villagers to respond to the goods and services that the project will provide. But sometimes things are not so simple. When this is the case, the capacity for adjustment can spell the difference between success and failure.

The Karonga/Chitipa IRD project in northern Malawi illustrates this point. Rice production in Karonga District was to be increased through the introduction of new varieties (Blue Bonnet and Blue Bell) and the use of improved cultivation practices. The traditional variety, Faya, was susceptible to breakage during milling and thus had little commercial value. But the people of the area loved Faya.

It was not hard to see why. A walk through the village in the evening was a sensory delight. The smell of Faya cooking over hardwood fires permeated the atmosphere and whetted the appetite. And the promise was fulfilled because Faya was a truly delicious variety that appealed to nearly all who tried it.

As a result, production of the improved varieties lagged behind targets. Villagers continued to plant Faya for household consumption and local sale. Although Faya did not respond to the new input package as well as did the new varieties, it retained the desired flavor and pleased the villagers.

The project and the Ministry of Agriculture accepted the farmers' values and attempted to arrive at a solution. Through research they developed a hybrid grain with milling characteristics of the new varieties while retaining the taste of Faya. It was called Superfaya.

In this case, success at promoting a behavioral response rested on the project's ability to meet beneficiary needs through a midcourse adjustment rather than assuming that the logic of a project technology would automatically induce the desired changes. To do this, flexibility and open communication are required.

The establishment of constructive channels of communication should begin during the needs analysis. If a participatory environment is not established from the beginning, it is more difficult to establish it later. IRD programs such as the Arusha project in Tanzania and PDP in Indonesia took special pains to involve villagers in the design and initiation of local subproject activities. On the whole, the effort paid off in enhanced local interest and response.

The most reliable means of finding out what the problems and felt needs of potential beneficiaries are is, simply, to ask them. This is not as obvious as it seems. Care must be taken to avoid producing an unrealistic wish list. Priorities must be established and consensus reached by soliciting the views of a wide spectrum of the local population: small-scale farmers, women, leaders, progressive farmers, civil servants, store owners, and merchants. Some constraints must also be considered: the government's development policies and priorities; the availability of personnel and resources; and the extent to which these felt needs are an expression of special interest groups rather than the local population as a whole.

Participation gives beneficiaries a stake in the project and thus an incentive to work as co-owners to make it succeed. This approach mixes incentives, risk sharing, and participatory management. But even more may be required. An illustration is provided by the Maasai project in Tanzania.

One objective of the project was to encourage increased marketing of cattle to satisfy the national demand for beef. But after the Maasai sold their cattle and obtained cash, they found that rural shops were empty of consumer goods. In fact, the principal item that could be bought was beer.

Forced social change with no replacement for eroded values and lost possessions did not improve well-being. As a result, there is little evidence that the response will be sustained. The project failed to meet the Maasai's needs. Economic circumstances and the policy environment did not offer an incentive for continued response.

However, one element of the project did meet beneficiary needs. The condition of the herd was visibly improved by dipping cattle to rid them of ticks. Although the Maasai were suspicious at first and resisted the new practice, the certainty of the technology, the speed of results, and the fit between those results and Maasai values led to swift adoption.

Generally, neither villagers' practical knowledge alone nor the technical knowledge of those introducing innovations is, of itself, sufficient to anticipate and overcome problems. A merging of both understandings is necessary to avoid the misapplication of new technologies and lessen the associated risks.

Sharing Risk

In rural areas, the government is often viewed by people as a tax collector and a provider of goods and services. Since government and project services are essentially free, there is little reason to value or care for them. A common manifestation of this attitude is the failure to repay government credit.

One notable initiative among IRD projects has been to incorporate a major finding of previous research and require some form of contribution toward project resources by beneficiaries.[37] That contribution was often in the form of labor but included money, facilities, and management.

Local resource commitment not only reduces needs for external contributions but, more important, also encourages owner-user identification with project goods and services. This identification, in turn, contributes to more honest project management, especially when an open management style is adopted. Furthermore, local maintenance of project products is substantially improved when local people view these products to be the result of their own efforts.

Resource commitments may be generated in a variety of ways, ranging from user's fees for services provided (as happens in many indigenous water-users' associations and cooperatives) to establishing some enterprise specifically devoted to raising funds for the local organization and its activities (such as a store, communal plot, moneylending organization, or labor pool). What is important is that participants control how these locally generated resources are allocated and used.

If possible, resource commitments should be made formal by a contract negotiated between beneficiaries and outside funding sources. This contractual arrangement takes beneficiary contributions seriously and provides increased local leverage. But these contracts must be negotiated so that local choice is retained and local capacity enhanced. The result will be better, more sustainable projects. This approach is a major step away from the creation of local dependency toward the support of local initiative, and it is on this initiative that authentic development depends.

Summary

The key to project success is local action, but all approaches that support it are not equally effective. Beneficiary studies, for example, have been largely unsuccessful as a result of their tendency to separate the knowledge gained through these studies from the political and administrative realities of implementation.

Although the use of local organizations has a spotty record, success invariably is associated with the use of local groups. Effective local organizations are characterized by control over a renewable resource base, broad-based membership, an open operating style, linkages to other organizations and sources of support, and a focus on a limited number of functions commensurate with the organization's experience and management strength.

Temporary subsidies, such as direct payment to farmers to adopt innovations or the granting of interest-free loans, tend to build local participation on a fragile, unsustainable base. This is a particular problem when subsidies are financed by foreign aid. Either these subsidies become a drain on the host government, or they cease at the end of project funding. In the first case, local dependency is perpetuated; in the second, purchased participation stops with the payments. Then the preproject conditions reassert themselves and project-introduced innovations remain only in memory and myth.

Poorly conceived project designs often fail to deal seriously with the risk considerations of the poor and other local factors that may restrain openness to innovation. Attempts to bypass landlords, merchants, and other nonpoor groups often result in project assumptions that are little more than imported myths and professional or political wishful thinking. The problem is compounded by complex designs that tend to lock local people out of the project decision process and move control into the hands of outside technical and administrative experts.

A participatory work environment encourages project staff to share resources and authority with clients and to develop a style of delivering services that emphasizes a collegial relationship with beneficiaries. But IRD experience with attempts to reorient bureaucracies to more open styles of management shows how hard this goal is to achieve. Structure is paramount. Political, bureaucratic, cultural, and donor incentives must support the use of resources to achieve development and social-learning objectives.

A key point is the need for technical staff to share resources and authority with beneficiaries. Thus, there is a basic contradiction between the need for concentrated authority to deliver services and the need for dispersed authority to encourage local action. A remaining question, then, is whether further contradictions emerge from consideration of the link between local action and long-run sustainability.

Notes

1. Grace Goodell, "Conservatism and Foreign Aid," Policy Review 19 (Winter 1982): 114.

2. Tracing the careers of bilateral aid mission directors gives an impression that particular types of projects begin to appear soon after the directors arrive at the new post. When this tendency combines with the fads that emanate from metropolitan centers, little room is left for local determination of program content. In East Africa, the phrase "Wazimu wa Mzungu" (the white man's madness), identified the proclivity of each new district commissioner to organize pet projects and ignore those of his predecessor. See J. Gus Liebenow, Political Development in Tanzania: The Case of the Makonde (Evanston, IL: Northwestern University Press, 1971). A malady of donor-driven development, then, is the mission director's madness.

3. Oleen Hess, The Establishment of Cattle Ranching Associations among the Masai in Tanzania, Occasional Paper no. 7 (Ithaca, NY: Cornell University, Rural Development Committee, 1976).

4. Frank J. Lynch et al., Let My People Lead (Institute of Philippine Culture, 1975).

5. See David C. Korten and George Carner, "Reorienting Bureaucracies to Serve People: Two Experiences from the Philippines," Canadian Journal Of Development Studies 5, no. 1 (1984): 7–24.

6. Charles W. Anderson, Political Factors in Latin American Economic Development (Madison, WI: University of Wisconsin, Land Tenure Center, 1966), 237–239.

7. Morgan J. Doughton, "People Power: An Alternative to Runaway Bureaucracy," The Futurist 14, no. 2 (April 1980): 18.

8. Fred O'Regan et al., Eliciting Needs in Planning Urban-Based Services for Rural Development (Washington, DC: The Development Group for Alternative Policies, March 1978), 66.

9. "Problems in Implementing the Integrated Development Project in Liberia," Audit Report no. 80–82 (Agency for International Development, 1980).

10. For background, see Arthur Goldsmith and Harvey Blustain, Local Organization and Participation in Integrated Development in Jamaica (Ithaca, NY: Cornell University, Rural Development Committee, 1980); and George Honadle, Fishing for Sustainability: The Role of Capacity Building in Development Administration, IRD Working Paper no. 8 (Washington, DC: Development Alternatives, Inc., 1981).

11. Many of the most active local social groupings are women's organizations. Often, these groups can take on functional tasks. In general, the propensity of rural women to organize and perform effectively in organizations is an often overlooked development resource.

12. Judith Tendler, Inter-Country Evaluation of Small Farmer Organizations (Washington, DC: Agency for International Development, Bureau for Latin America, Office of Development Programs, 1976), 9.

13. See John D. Montgomery, "The Populist Front in Rural Development: Or Shall We Eliminate the Bureaucrats and Get on with the Job," Public Administration Review 39, no. 1 (1979).

14. See especially Norman T. Uphoff and Milton J. Esman, Local Organization for Rural Development: Analysis of Asian Experience (Ithaca, NY: Cornell University, Rural Development Committee, November 1974); Norman T. Uphoff, Providing for More Participation in Project Planning and Implementation, draft (Ithaca, NY: Cornell University, Rural Development Committee, 1981); and, in summary form, Arthur A. Goldsmith and Harvey S. Blustain, Local Organization and Participation, 7–11.

15. A. H. Barclay, Jr. and Gary Eilerts, Institutional Options for the Mandara Area Development Project, IRD Field Report no. 11 (Washington, DC: Development Alternatives, Inc., 1980), 20–32.

16. A. H. Barclay, Jr. et al., Internal Evaluation of the North Shaba Project (Washington, DC: Development Alternatives, Inc., November 1980), 15–30.

17. David D. Gow and Jerry VanSant, "Beyond the Rhetoric of Rural Development Participation: How Can it Be Done?," World Development 11, no. 5 (1983): 6.

18. David C. Korten and Norman T. Uphoff, *Bureaucratic Reorientation for Rural Development* (Manila, Philippines, and Ithaca, NY: Asian Institute of Management and Cornell University, Rural Development Committee, 1981), 3.

19. Goodell, "Conservatism and Foreign Aid," 111, 118.

20. Jerry VanSant et al., *Management Support to the Jamaican Ministry of Agriculture Second Integrated Rural Development Project*, IRD Field Report no. 13 (Washington, DC: Development Alternatives, Inc., 1981).

21. Albert O. Hirschman, *Development Projects Observed* (Washington, DC: The Brookings Institution, 1967), 151.

22. John M. Cohen, *The Administration of Economic Development Programs: Baselines for Discussion* (Cambridge, MA: Harvard Institute for International Development, October 1979), 66.

23. Robert Chambers, "Project Selection for Poverty Focussed Rural Development: Simple Is Optimal," *World Development* 6, no. 2 (1978): 209–219.

24. *Ibid.*, 210.

25. See Charles F. Sweet and Peter F. Weisel, "Process versus Blueprint Models for Designing Rural Development Projects," in George Honadle and Rudi Klauss, eds., *International Development Administration: Implementation Analysis for Development Projects* (New York: Praeger, 1979).

26. Robert Chambers and Mick Howes, "Rural Development: Whose Knowledge Counts?" *IDS Bulletin* 10, no. 2 (1979).

27. Derick Brinkerhoff, "Inside Public Bureaucracy: Empowering Managers to Empower Clients," *Rural Development Participation Review* 1, no. 1 (1979): 7–9.

28. George Honadle, "Structural Aspects of Capacity Building, or Who Gets the Fish?," *Rural Development Participation Review*, 3, no. 3 (1982), special supplement, pp. 1–3.

29. Jerry VanSant and Peter F. Weisel, *Community Based Integrated Rural Development (CBIRD) in the Special Territory of Aceh, Indonesia*, IRD Field Report no. 4 (Washington, DC: Development Alternatives, Inc., 1979). For an account of similar experience in South Korea, see Phillip Coombs, ed., *Meeting the Basic Needs of the Rural Poor: The Integrated Community-Based Approach* (New York: Pergamon Press, 1980).

30. Gow and VanSant, "Beyond the Rhetoric."

31. See, for example, William G. Scott and David K. Hart, *Organizational America* (Boston, MA: Houghton Mifflin, 1979).

32. See, for example, Frances F. Korten, *Building National Capacity to Develop Water User Associations: Experience from the Philippines*, World Bank Staff Working Paper no. 528, 1982.

33. See Korten and Uphoff, *Bureaucratic Reorientation*.

34. David D. Gow, *An Information System for the Rural Area Development – Rapti Zone Project*, IRD Field Report no. 8 (Washington, DC: Development Alternatives, Inc., 1980).

35. Elliott R. Morss, "The Arusha Planning and Village Development Project: An Assessment of Participation at Two Levels," *Rural Development Participation Review* 3, no. 3 (1982), special supplement, 11–13.

36. George Honadle, "Supervising Agriculture Extension: Practices and Procedures for Improving Field Performance," *Agricultural Administration* 9, no. 1 (1982).

37. See Gow and VanSant, "Beyond the Rhetoric."

CHAPTER FOUR

Sustaining Benefits

L ocal action in response to project initiatives is one key to success. But if the action does not lead to the actor's betterment, then it is not likely to be sustained. Unmarketed produce does not raise farmer income, nor does it provide an incentive to continue planting that crop.

Unfortunately, the IRD experience is filled with examples of the withering away of hard-earned gains from project activities. Sometimes climatic shifts, such as droughts, hasten the retreat from success. Other times, however, the cause is more closely related to the ill-conceived or incomplete strategies followed by development planners and supporters.

In East Africa, for example, expatriate scientists worked nearly 15 years to develop better varieties of maize. But when the last technicians left in the mid-1970s, research ground to a halt. Although technical assistance had been provided, institutional capacity to continue had not been built. Unfortunately, this is an all too common fate.

Most IRD strategies cast production, whether of roads or crops, as the star in the development drama. Concern for sustaining that production by maintaining physical or institutional infrastructure is left for supporting actors. The result is an implementation style that pays lip service to sustaining functions and benefits while yielding the resources and the spotlight to immediate production. Thus, this chapter is concerned with factors that are too often viewed as complementary or supporting rather than as central.

At the same time, the dreary record of unsustained advances was well known before the IRD projects reviewed in this book were designed. In fact, all of them contained components, or made assumptions, that were directed toward sustaining the initiatives of the project. To appreciate the lessons of that experience, one must understand the logic of outside intervention and induced change, identify the major constraints to sustained benefit flows, and determine what strategies the IRD projects used to ensure long-term results.

Logic of Intervention

Induced rural development assumes that outside resources can be used to provide a push to local action and the marshaling of local resources. It assumes that if a new technology is introduced people will use it, take charge of their own destiny, and begin a self-sustaining development process.

The linear flow from resources to improved well-being and capability is only the initial phase. A more accurate rendition would show the project as providing just a nudge to a cycle in which an increase in the resources available locally would make new goods and services available, induce response, and then generate a greater resource base. An analogy might be the ignition of a diesel engine—a project acts as a starter motor. This perspective is displayed in Figure 3. The key element, however, is the transition from starter motor to main engine.

Projects, by definition, are time bound. One way or another, they end. Therefore, planning for projects tends to be equally time bound in focus. The end of a project is logically seen as a termination, but it is actually just a beginning. What begins, if anything, at project end is ultimately more important than the project itself; what continues represents the real contribution of the project.

In this context, every planning and implementation decision should be made in the light of the sustainability issue. An emphasis on immediate production goals leads to project designs, organizational choices, and management practices that block any chances for turnover. The transition from starter motor to main engine never takes place.

One example of this situation occurred in the Second Integrated Rural Development Project (IRDP II) in Jamaica. This project was conceived and begun as a major soil conservation effort. Later, it added a focus on local farmer organizations. Then it recognized the need for an integrated extension-marketing strategy if production and income targets were to be attained. The result was a disorganized mix of objectives in search of a common approach. Adding to the difficulty was the lack of effort made to develop indicators of farm welfare in the project area, or to measure impact beyond the achievement of physical component targets.

A primary measure of project performance was the completion of farm plans for those farmers participating in this watershed-oriented effort. Management emphasized the development of new plans at the expense of follow-up with those farmers already enrolled in the program. The threat to sustainability is obvious— the transition from project activity to a more permanent set of actors requires that they have the resources, knowledge, and desire to continue local action. But in this project, it was not known what levels of staffing (if any) could be maintained by the Jamaican government or whether any special project services, such as extension outreach in marketing, credit, and home economics, would be continued. Since project watershed boundaries were not contiguous with those of Jamaican political jurisdictions, and there was no resource base for a special district, administrative continuity of any kind was unlikely.

Project staff were aware of the difficulties, but the focus on immediate production targets caused them to ignore what would happen after the project

FIGURE 3

INTERVENTION TO PROMOTE SELF-RELIANCE

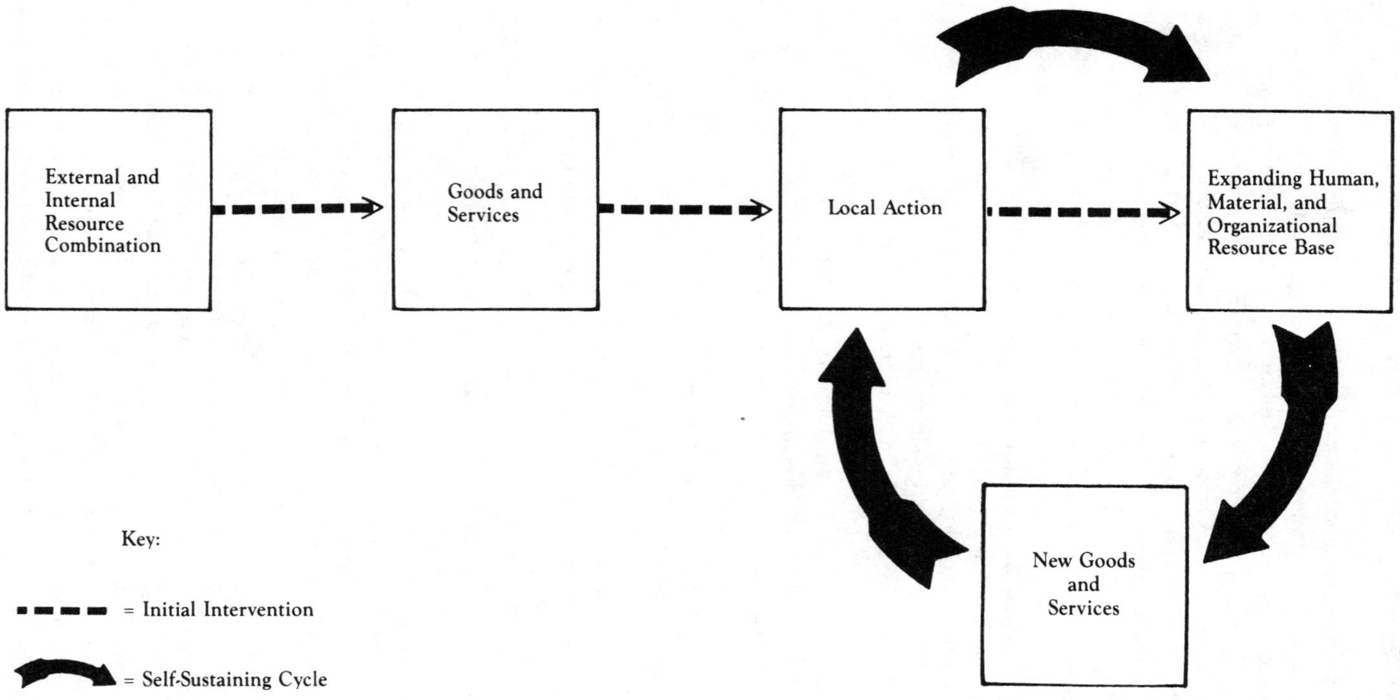

External and Internal Resource Combination

Goods and Services

Local Action

Expanding Human, Material, and Organizational Resource Base

New Goods and Services

Key:

= Initial Intervention

= Self-Sustaining Cycle

terminated. The emphasis was on immediate action at the expense of the transition to a sustained local effort.

The need for this transition places great importance on the resource control, perceptions, and general situation of local people. In Mbeya Region of Tanzania in the 1960s, for example, the word "serikali" was used to describe the local cooperatives.[1] Since this is the Swahili word for government, it suggested that these organizations were seen as arms of the central government rather than as controlled by the villagers. Not realizing this fact could easily lead development planners astray in their search for an organizational host for a development effort in the area. Thus, knowledge of rural people's interpretations of their circumstances is a key element in ensuring the sustainability of interventions supported by outsiders.

Similarly, the unwillingness of some Indonesian villagers to band together and rebuild a bridge destroyed by a flood was criticized by an outsider. However, the lack of action was not the result of fatalism. Instead, it derived from power relationships within the community. As long as the bridge remained unmended, those who had boats would profit by ferrying people across the river. Since the village headman benefited by having relatives provide the service, there was a vested interest in delaying the reconstruction of the bridge. Strategies for achieving sustainability, then, must be well grounded in the context of local decision making, and they must be based on an awareness of local constraints.

Constraints to Sustainability

Choice of an inappropriate technology is often touted as a major cause of failure in development programs. But the IRD record suggests that the technology itself is only part of the problem. The difficulty also lies with the support system required by the technology, or with the administrative focus on immediate production to the exclusion of longer-term institutional, environmental, and cultural concerns.

These issues may be separated into four major categories: financial constraints, organizational constraints, policy constraints, and side effects. Each category is discussed below.

Financial Constraints

Projects often fail to induce sustainable processes as a result of financial factors. High-cost subsidized goods and services are used without generating the ability to cover the cost of maintaining and replacing them. Thus, the possibility that these goods and services will continue to be provided after outside funding ends is reduced or eliminated.

Project planners sometimes design projects as though the availability of donor funds and host country resources were unlimited. And this tendency is reinforced by pressure on donors to use foreign assistance and capital-intensive solutions.

Many developing countries also express a preference for more sophisticated capital equipment than is needed. In fact, they often view the infrastructure dimensions of a project as the most important.

Technicians trained in developed countries also prefer to use familiar methods and state-of-the-art equipment. One evaluation of the United States Agency for International Development (AID), for example, observed that a rural roads project in the Philippines had a strong bias toward sophisticated methods that emphasized capital-intensive construction and excluded community participation as a result of the availability of excess U.S. equipment at artificially low prices.[2] Similarly, excessive costs result from trying to do too much too soon.

Although the recurrent cost needs of an individual project may not seem excessive, the aggregate demand for recurrent funds implicit in a large number of donor projects may become a severe burden. For example, the fiscal year 1983 AID Country Development Strategy Statement for Upper Volta noted that the total recurrent cost burden imposed on the Government of Burkina Faso budget by AID-sponsored projects will be almost one quarter of the projected national budget by 1987. Burkina Faso will be unable to finance these costs from anticipated revenues. A similar situation has already arisen in Tanzania, where the government is in default on development loans, many of which were provided through donor-supported project investments.

This problem is exacerbated when the true costs of a project are hidden. For example, one feature of the Indonesia Provincial Area Development Program (PDP) in the province of Nusa Tenggara Timur was the construction of food-storage buildings to serve several nearby villages. Previously, farmers were forced by market conditions to sell their produce at depressed harvest-time prices and later to repurchase it for personal needs at dry-season prices, which could be double or triple what they received earlier. The PDP warehouses, in contrast, planned to buy the produce at a fair price and resell with a modest markup to cover costs of the warehouse staff and routine maintenance. Thus, the farmer incurred a reasonable cost for the service of storage.

But, in reality, it was a PDP-subsidized cost because the markup did not include any allowance for amortizing the cost of warehouse construction. These subsidies helped ensure that the warehouses could offer a better deal than outside traders, but the subsidies did not help to build a sustainable system. It appears that, in the future absence of outside funding, existing warehouses will fall into disrepair and no new ones will be built as a result of the lack of an institutionalized source of capital. If, in contrast, depreciation costs had been included in the markup, then a sustainable system might have been created because farmers would have paid real costs and would have been able to judge the merits of the system. Of course, if the resulting markups led to a system that was non-competitive with the traders, then the whole concept would be best abandoned anyway. Few things work more against the possibility of sustained response than hidden subsidies.

In this example, realistic treatment of costs in pricing services would have had the effect of transferring some benefits from the individual beneficiaries of the project back into the system so that it might be sustained or even expanded. There are many ways a portion of revenue may be recycled to maintain the benefit flow—fees for services; realistic interest rates on loans; or some agreed-on return of a percentage of project-related production or income gains, when these are readily quantifiable.

Often, however, the impact of development expenditures on recurrent costs are underestimated. More political capital accrues to a local government for providing new facilities than for maintaining existing ones. This emphasis on capital stock makes it that much more difficult to consider adequately the financial constraints to sustainability.

Moreover, just as donors have often succumbed to an edifice complex, so too recipients commonly equate the proliferation of modern infrastructure with development. Sustainability yields to visibility unless organizational pressures can prevent this from happening. Thus, what economists have labeled the recurrent cost problem is simply a symptom of a deeper failing—a lack of supportive institutional response to project initiatives.

Organizational Constraints

Few project ideas are so compelling that they will perpetuate benefits without organizations equipped to carry them forward. Usually, the organizations must be created or strengthened during the implementation process. When external resources end, local actors must be able to continue activities, often with fewer resources than before. Institutional capacity, therefore, is a key element in project sustainability.

In many projects, however, relatively little emphasis is given to the problems of institutionalization, institution building, and training. Indeed, projects are often designed to avoid the need to build capacity. The creation of special project management units (PMUs), divorced from the regular host government bureaucracies, for example, is a favored implementation approach of large donor agencies. This bypass approach is often justified on the grounds that existing institutions are too weak to implement planned activities and achieve their objectives within the required life of the project.

Autonomy avoids many bureaucratic constraints that can hinder a project, and it can ensure a greater accountability to the donor over the resources and funds spent. Moreover, PMUs, because they are independent of the country's civil service system, can pay higher salaries and attract more capable staff than would otherwise be possible. Often, however, these individuals come from ministerial positions where they are also needed. Thus, a temporary device initially created to bypass institutional weaknesses actually exacerbates them. Furthermore, because of the isolation of IRD projects, PMUs have little effect on the performance of permanent institutions.

Incentives must also exist for local hosts to do what is necessary to deliver benefits. Project activities may result in bureaucratic opposition that undermines the continuation of the project and the sustainability of its benefits. This was the case, for example, with an AID-funded agricultural research project in Thailand. There, the Ministry of Agriculture and Cooperatives (MOAC) initially supported the creation of a regional agricultural research center, even though it was to be housed in another agency. However, MOAC officials soon viewed the research center as a competitor for resources (budgets, personnel, and external aid), and their initial enthusiasm for the project died. As long as AID controlled budgetary funds for training, research equipment, and commodities, open political maneuvering against the project was restrained. When AID's role in the project ended, however, the opponents of the research center moved openly against its budget and mandate, and it was subsequently stripped of most of its resources and authority. Thus, institutional incentives militated against sustained benefit delivery. They promoted the dismantling of project resources and the rejection of project innovations.

Similarly, the sustainability of Liberia's Lofa County Integrated Agricultural Development Project was adversely affected by incentives not to build capacity. The PMU was supposed to build up cooperatives and then dissolve, leaving them in control. But the cooperatives have not become self-sustaining. In fact, from the project's inception the PMU concentrated on developing its own ability to provide services to farmers, rather than on strengthening the cooperatives' ability to assume responsibility for those services.

Political constraints to the creation of sustainable cooperatives were numerous. First, the cooperatives were controlled by the wealthy and powerful, whom the farmers did not fully trust. Second, the middlemen were resistant to the cooperatives. These individuals had leverage because they were moneylenders as well and could stop providing banking services to the people, a function the cooperatives were not able to carry out. Third, the Liberian Produce Marketing Corporation was a relatively strong elite-run agency, which would have been displaced by a build-up of cooperatives. Thus, opposition was mounted from various directions.

Inadequate capacity, then, is often a reflection of inadequate incentives. Scarce resources combined with institutional competition may create an environment that will thwart most attempts at capacity building.

Policy Constraints

All development projects exist within national political and economic settings that affect their performance and potential. Indeed, the chances for success are low for even a carefully designed and well-implemented project when it exists in an unfavorable political and economic environment.[3]

Development problems frequently result from the interaction of several policies. A typical example from Africa involves price controls and high export duties on domestic agricultural products. Both policies favor urban populations over rural groupings and are frequently imposed to attain this distributional effect. In other instances, a combination of policies will be used to bring about stabilization. One Asian government, for example, severely devalued its currency at the urging of the International Monetary Fund. However, it failed to adjust its rice procurement price to offset the increased price of agricultural imports such as fertilizer. Normally, farmers could have sold their produce on the unregulated market. However, the limited capacity of grain storage facilities in the private sector prohibited the level of market demand at harvest time that was needed to create an adequate return to the farmer.

Other examples of macro policy at odds with area project objectives and influencing local response may be cited. In Bolivia, a national policy of subsidized interest rates and lax repayment requirements have principally benefited large farmers and limited the supply of capital for small farmer credit programs. Currency exchange regulations in Zaire encouraged imports of food into a food-deficit area while a project attempted to increase local food production. In Ethiopia and Indonesia, import restrictions and free-market controls aggravated the storage of critical project inputs such as fertilizer and spare parts. This in turn limited project effectiveness at the district, community, and village levels.

Developing countries have historically suffered from serious economic problems such as shortages of domestic savings and hard currency, as well as internal demand and supply imbalances. These difficulties have led, in turn, to slow growth, unemployment, and high rates of inflation.[4] In many cases, governments chose, or were forced, to address these problems in ways that inadvertently hampered the implementation or impact of projects. This was the case, for example, with the failure of a project to construct a rice mill in Papua New Guinea. When the government lowered the official price for rice, the farmers in the region no longer found it profitable to market their output. Consequently, they switched from rice to other crops. The newly constructed government rice mill had been built based on assumptions that were no longer reasonable. As a result, the mill eventually went bankrupt.

Macroeconomic policies can impinge on both implementation and sustainability. Domestic price ceilings, designed to promote exports and maintain low food prices in urban areas, often lower or eliminate the incentives for farmers to increase production or adopt agricultural innovations. Import tariffs or quotas to foster domestic production of agricultural inputs may increase production costs and lower incentives to increase production. Foreign exchange controls may restrict the importation of critical inputs, such as fuel, needed to continue project activities. For example, a project in a West African country was prohibited from importing light-weight plows in favor of heavier, domestically produced ones. However, the heavier plows were poorly adapted to the soils in the project area and had to be pulled by oxen, rather than less expensive donkeys. As a result, there was little demand for the project-supplied plows.[5]

Restrictive monetary policies can limit the access of beneficiaries to credit, and tight budget restrictions may lead to shortages in personnel and administrative support. Unless projects are designed with these macroeconomic limitations in mind, or the policies themselves are changed by the host governments, the success of development projects and the sustainability of the benefits they generate will continue to be undermined.

Economic policies may support development projects, but in ways that cannot be sustained. For example, the reliance on a technological package requiring the heavy use of chemical fertilizer may not be sustainable in a country in which fertilizer is imported using scarce foreign exchange, or where the rural infrastructure is inadequate to ensure its timely distribution.

A parallel market for project outputs can also obstruct project objectives and threaten sustainability. In the Niger Cereals Production Project, for example, a seed multiplication effort was failing because of the low official price and high parallel market price for grain. Rather than delivering the new seed to the project, the farmers who contracted to mass produce it sold the seed for twice the official price to buyers smuggling it into Nigeria, where it was consumed rather than planted.[6]

A political policy of particular significance to rural development is agrarian reform. Its proponents argue that it is essential to increased agricultural development. Equity arguments aside, it is thought that title security and intensive production, both of which are seen as resulting from a meaningful agrarian reform, will lead to significant production and income increases. Two problems with agrarian reform policies warrant further attention. First, there is the danger that these policies, implemented in a country with rapid growth, will result in such a high degree of land fragmentation that small holdings become uneconomic.

Second, there are transition costs in any agrarian reform. Production declines as the new landholders take charge. These declines can be large when the transition period is stretched out, when it occurs through violence, or when the reform is poorly conceived or implemented. Moreover, unforeseen side effects can negate the reform. Even so, agrarian reform is often an essential element for sustained equitable development—when the tillers of the land cannot keep its bounty, they have no reason to conserve, improve, or even continue to till it.

The political distance between central planners and local people frequently manifests itself in project designs that are imbued with a lack of knowledge about local conditions and a lack of accountability to local people. Since resources also tend to be centrally controlled, the result is often a portfolio of national policies and implementation strategies that serve other than rural interests and that culminate in efforts with detrimental side effects.

Side Effects as Constraints

Despite careful planning and expert management, IRD projects may produce many effects that are neither planned nor foreseen. Unanticipated effects are usually perceived as negative, although positive side effects may also occur. One observer's review of project experience in the 1960s identified "the centrality of side effects."[7] Although they may not always assume this much importance, side effects certainly can pose strong threats to sustainability.

Many unanticipated project effects result from social, economic, and technological changes that accompany the investment of project funds, delivery of goods and services, and stimulation of responses in a community. The resulting transformation can severely disrupt the traditional order. The established distribution of power and wealth, and existing social stratification, have a stability that interventions upset, either intentionally or accidentally. In the aftermath, alternative social organizations that are timely and adequate are seldom provided. The resulting social disruption is a likely source of negative side effects.

A case in point is the agrarian reform issue noted above. Land, in many societies, is not just a commodity. Instead, it is a focal point for a complex set of human interactions. When outsiders misinterpret the nature of these interactions and fail to understand who gets what from them, then those outsiders are apt to prescribe courses of action that lead down unintended pathways.

For example, poor farmers in the Philippines have sometimes been made worse off by land tenure reforms that were presumably intended to improve their lot. Under the traditional system, a sharecropper received assistance from the landowner when the former's house was destroyed by a typhoon. Since the new system of freehold title dissolved the patron-client relationship, the rural poor lost this assistance. In many areas, a house was wrecked about every five years, and thus this was no small service lost.

The foundation for a policy of breaking up estates and converting tenants to owners made sense at the time—tenants could not be expected to risk scarce capital for inputs or increase their labor using new methods if most proceeds went to the landlord. The problem, however, is that outside observers often mistake anchor chains for prison chains. That is, what appears to an outsider as a constraint to accumulating material wealth or implementing a specific policy may appear to insiders as a price that they will willingly pay for a different social privilege, material good, or religious comfort.

From the indigenous calculus, the tradeoffs may be worthwhile. Thus, a shallow understanding of the social system surrounding a resource often leads to false judgments about the implications of new uses for it. Side effects may block sustainability, either temporarily or permanently.

Side effects may be physical as well as social. In a potable water project, for example, health benefits can accrue from an increased volume of water or they can result from its improved quality. But if net benefits are not as great as expected, the reason may stem from burdens resulting from contamination. The availability of the water may even produce environmental degradation, resulting in a situation worse than that before the project began. The reduction of soil fertility as a result of the intrusion of a dam, or an increase in schistosomiasis due to the introduction of irrigated production practices, is among the many consequences of IRD programs in such places as Liberia.[8]

Figure 4 illustrates the complexity of the benefits and burdens that can be expected as a result of a potable water project. The foundation for this benefit tree is IRD experience in Tanzania.

Strategies For Achieving Sustainability

The preceding constraints to sustainability were not always addressed directly by the projects reviewed in this book. Even so, all the projects had either definite strategies or specific assumptions related to the prospects for long-term success. These strategies and assumptions may be grouped into three categories— institutional, organizational, and technological.

Often projects simultaneously embodied two or more of these approaches. In fact, different components were usually designed to pursue each strategy, some at a program level and some at the project level. Selected field experiences exemplify the way success and failure with any particular approach varied with local circumstances and the project's ability to deal with a complex web of constraints.

Institutional Strategies

An institutional strategy emphasizes the need for large-scale pre-existing institutions to assume project responsibilities. Some projects fail because they cannot institutionalize new functions and the capacity to carry them out within government bodies. For example, the need for rural representation in national policy making and for a permanent mechanism to coordinate rural development were to be addressed by a rural development authority in Liberia, but the fate of that effort was sealed in interministerial combat (see Chapter 3 for details).

A more successful experience is represented by the Bicol River Basin Development Program Office in the Philippines. Here a regional planning, monitoring, and coordinating unit was established before projects were developed. Its function was not to execute development projects, but to offer design and support services to the line ministries implementing IRD projects in the region. A strong staff from the area was assembled and trained, and long-run resources were obtained through the acquisition of a line item in the national budget. Most important, however, the unit acquired a place in the local institutional landscape by augmenting, rather than competing with, the agendas, priorities, and programs of the line agencies. Rather than displacing the ministries, it strengthened the regional offices in their competition with other areas for the ministerial budget. The difference between the Liberian and Philippine examples is a key determinant for explaining the different levels of success.

Strengthening of governmental machinery also characterized projects dealing with subnational units, such as PDP in Indonesia and the Arusha Planning and

FIGURE 4

DIRECT AND SIDE EFFECTS OF NEW POTABLE WATER SOURCE

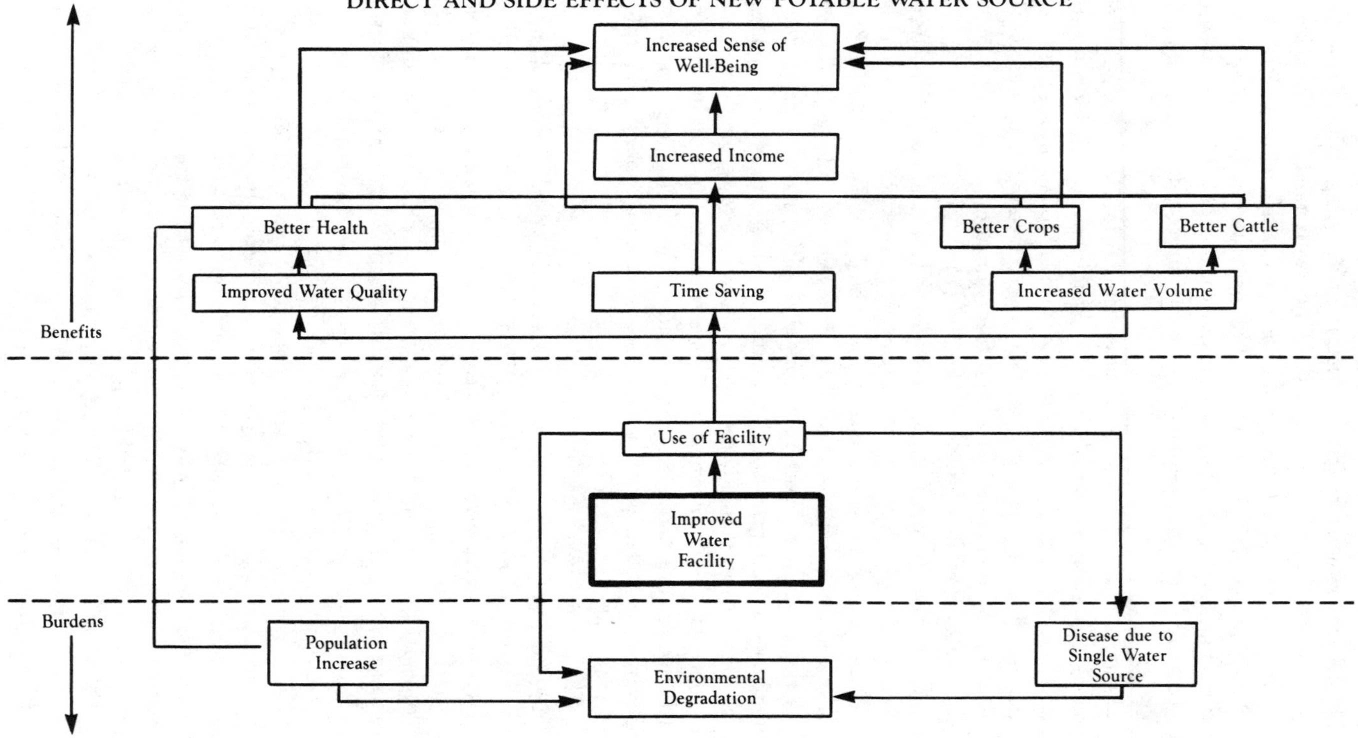

Village Development Project in Tanzania. Training, critical examination of bureaucratic procedures, and experimentation with subprojects were key elements in these programs. In addition, they were program-level interventions and not just single projects. The need to build capacity within a permanent institution in the public sector was seen as necessary to achieve sustained development in the country. This goal required a program strategy instead of a pure project orientation.

When a pure project approach was taken, institutional strengthening seldom resulted. For example, IRDP II in Jamaica encountered difficulty in finding revenue sources to cover recurrent costs as well as to continue supporting project initiatives after the end of external funding. An inability to address the larger environment certainly limited any prospects for sustainability—the use of a PMU precluded successful institutional strengthening.

Also integral to an institutional strategy was a focus on policy reform. Examining institutional incentives and the context of decentralization often highlighted policy inconsistencies or obstacles to new objectives. Topics such as pricing policies, interregional equity, marketing arrangements, and legal restrictions on revenue generation all emerged as concerns of IRD implementers.[9] Even though these issues arose, and projects sometimes had organizational linkages to high levels, in the short run only regional deviations were accomplished. Experience in Indonesia, the Philippines, and Zaire supports this conclusion. Sometimes small changes did take place at the national level. In Tanzania, for example, innovations in incentive allowances became national policy.[10] But this was rare and marginal.

The general weakness of vertical linkages was a contributory factor in this failing of IRD, especially when the projects used PMUs. Seldom did micro change induce macro change, but this situation resulted more from the rigidity of those macro systems themselves than from poor project performance. Control-oriented civil service regulations, chaotic decision making, and oppressive political use of bureaucratic machinery were not easily remedied by expanding a practice introduced into a single field location. In fact, they were seldom influenced at all.

Recent emphasis on the private sector has been advanced as one way around this blockage. The assumption that ownership is the primary determinant of behavior, however, is not always supported by experience. Thus, the private sector focus should not be accepted unquestioningly. For some functions, in some places, it makes sense. The danger is that emphasis on the private sector will become another nonworking panacea rather than an option with selective potential. In Zaire, for example, it is sometimes hard to identify just what falls into which sector.[11] The public purse is often found in private pockets.

Based on work with IRD and policy analysis in Egypt and the Philippines, one observer has suggested a way around system rigidities. If institutional capacity is separated into the ability to do something (internal capacity) versus the ability to get something done by someone else (process capacity), the strengthening of the ability of public institutions to obtain services from private organizations can receive more emphasis.[12] This process-capacity approach is appealing in many circumstances, and it implies a dual effort, bringing public and private actors together to improve overall performance by refocusing bureaucratic attention.

In general, bureaucratic reorientation was not a central tenet in the IRD scripture. When the environment in a developing country was seen as hostile to a target group of intended beneficiaries called the rural poor, there was a tendency not to pursue a strategy of improving the effectiveness of formal public sector units. Instead, the building of villager organizations was seen as a way out of the governmental trap.

Organizational Strategies

An organizational strategy creates new small-scale organizations to carry on project activities. Establishing villager organizations and then devolving responsibility for selected project functions to them is a common IRD strategy for avoiding the problems of recurrent cost and institutional inadequacy within the public sector. At the same time, organizational strategies share a central element with institutional approaches — the preparation of those who will inherit project functions, assets, and liabilities to execute the functions, care for the assets, and discharge the liabilities. Capacity building within project-initiated inheritor groups, then, is the keystone of organizational strategies. Theoretically, the image of self-reliance and local equity that accompanies this approach is appealing. But the record suggests that the way it is implemented often thwarts the goal.

The timing of a transition from project operation of a facility to local control, for example, may affect the ability of a farmer association to assume responsibility and perform effectively. A study in the Bicol region of the Philippines showed this is the case in an irrigation facility that was to be turned over to a farmer organization.[13] At certain times of the year, the organization would experience a severe cash-flow problem and could not operate without assistance. At other times, however, the organization would have a surplus and no difficulty assuming the financial burdens of the system's operations.

Thus, timing was one element of the way IRD implementation influenced the effectiveness of this strategy. Another element was the degree of resource concentration or dispersion. Seldom was a concerted effort put into one beneficiary organization. Instead, technical assistance and resources were spread out among numerous small and geographically removed groups. The result was that none achieved the critical mass of resources and skills needed to perform well. The development effort was diluted rather than concentrated. This was the case in such countries as Indonesia, Jamaica, and Liberia. When things did go well, such as in the National Irrigation Administration in the Philippines[14] and in the Save the Children Community Based Integrated Rural Development Project in Indonesia,[15] the emphasis on one focal organization was present.

The inability to concentrate effort resulted from both design and management factors. Political pressure to include many locations in a project often produced designs that scattered the focus. Since project designs were often the result of compromises among the various actors, multiple agendas frequently led to a diluted strategy. At the same time, those pressures did not cease with the beginning of implementation – they just moved to a new arena. When this situation was combined with the sheer inability of field-level project managers to set priorities and order the sequence of activities, the effect was a further erosion of the capacity-building effort.

During implementation, administrative interpretations of policy objectives can also make a difference, especially if multiple objectives are pursued. A case in point was identified in Indonesia.

An explicit objective of an Indonesian government's five-year plan was equity. Expenditure per province was allocated on a per capita basis with an instruction to reach the poorest segments of the population. The implementation of this objective, however, made the prospects for sustainability questionable.

To achieve equitable distribution of funds over the entire island of Madura during the plan period, local administrators divided the villages not yet receiving direct assistance into three groups, with each village to receive help during only one of the three remaining years of the plan. A PDP-funded gardening subproject fell victim to this approach.

The gardening project was established with a revolving fund to pay for the costs of two new extension agents. A percentage of the revenues generated by vegetable sales would pay for inputs, while another portion would replace the funds used to pay the agents' salaries. The rest would remain with the growers.

To keep the revolving fund solvent, slightly more than 50 percent of the growers would have to achieve a specific production level. The actual success rate, however, was less than 35 percent. This rate was not bad when a learning curve is taken into account. But the rule requiring extension agents to move on to new villages each year potentially guaranteed that the target would not be reached, the learning curve would not be climbed, the fund would not revolve, and the extension services would not pay for themselves.

In this case, an administrative interpretation of an equity objective produced the dispersion of resources that made sustainability less probable. Compounding this problem of scattered effort was a phenomenon that might be called the new development machismo. That is, the proof that a project was reaching the rural poor was related to the difficulty of access to the project site – the more kilometers of bumpy trail, the more fords of flooding rivers, the more hours in small boats, the more hills climbed, or the more days walking to the project location the better the project and the more status accorded to those providing technical assistance.

This attitude may be good if it protects beneficiaries from predatory groups that might otherwise siphon off benefits. But as part of a larger effort, it may make management of the project almost impossible. When scarce management or technical assistance talent spends most of its time either traveling among remote sites or recuperating from the effects of the travel, little capacity gets built.

Although technical assistance and training were common features of projects using the organizational strategy to achieve sustainability, IRD field experience suggests that they are not always appropriate or sufficient. A combination of seven elements, however, does appear to signal a high chance of success. Five of these are process factors; the other two are substantive, or structural, in nature.[16]

The first process characteristic is a collaborative style. This characteristic is well documented and needs no further elaboration here. The relationship between providers and receivers of technical assistance affects degrees of trust, client commitment to recommendations, and mutual learning.

The second process element is an emphasis on learning how to make things work and to solve and define problems rather than relying on a predetermined technology or solution. Successful programs are able to generate an excitement about engaging in a learning process.

Collaboration and learning are closely linked because of two dimensions necessary to the learning process—engagement and reflection. Engagement involves learning by doing, enlightenment through action. Analysis, abstraction, and prescription are not enough. Unless those who build capacity are willing to become players in the drama, they are not likely to succeed. Their immersion demonstrates a collaborative spirit and reinforces how little they, as outsiders, actually know about the harsh realities. The learning process is mutual, and it is in the fires of organizational battles that truly collaborative ties are forged.

Reflection is equally necessary. Activity will implicitly define capacity, and unless objectives are made explicit and scrutinized, larger issues will be lost. Moreover, engagement without reflection may produce euphoria over apparent but actually superficial progress, while more important structural obstacles are missed and possibly even reinforced.

The three other process elements are closely linked to the first two: risk sharing, the involvement of multiple levels, and an emphasis on demonstration. Risk sharing is needed because there is a greater chance that innovations will become self-sustaining and that client commitment will be high when the client and service provider share the risk of failure. The involvement of multiple levels of actors is one outcome of projects funded by several donors. But it is intrinsically important. Attempts to bypass local leaders or senior staff and deal only with small-scale farmers or junior staff are bound to be nonsustainable. If the capabilities of extension staff are to be improved, for example, supervisory personnel and project leadership should be involved. If they do not support intended behavior, there is little chance that initial changes will continue. Thus, capacity-building activities that focus only on one organizational or societal level may be expected to falter. Unless higher levels are incorporated into the capacity-building process, the existing power structure can block changes that threaten that structure.

The final process element is demonstration. Unless new behaviors are demonstrably more effective than old ones, skeptical farmers or civil servants will not adopt them. The success of the green revolution has been largely the result of the ability to show the superiority of new technologies. This also implies that, when training is a major component of a capacity-enhancing program, it too should be of demonstrable value. Thus, the training should involve actual groups working on real problems and not be based on artificial exercises with participants drawn from all corners of the globe.

Although these five process considerations are important, structural barriers can negate even the best executed processes. The first structural consideration, incentives, has already been discussed. The second is the resource base.

The local resource base includes indigenous technical knowledge, community folk-management skills, and informal networks used to make things happen. But it has a physical and financial aspect as well as a human and organizational one. In instances in which physical and financial resources already exist, so much the better. In the more frequent case in which a new resource base is provided (whether through increased income from agricultural production or local taxing power, for example), the source and reliability of the new base must be examined carefully. For example, if taxing power is to be given to a village-level entity, the certainty of the citizenry's future income and the predatory inclinations of higher government levels must be evaluated in measuring the adequacy of future revenue for village projects.

In addition, the nature of the resources themselves should be considered. Project-related capitalization for a cooperative or a line item in a provincial budget, for example, is not a reliable source of funding for an organization without previous power. However, a monopoly over physical resources such as irrigation water, wells, a forestry preserve, or a village woodlot provides a much sounder financial basis for future activities.

In fact, it can be hypothesized that an essential element of successful capacity building in nondominant groups is the acquisition of control over a central set of natural resources. Thus, capacity-building efforts based only on providing social services or improving management practices are unlikely to be sustainable. Success commonly requires a link to income-producing activity and sufficient control over the disposition of that income.

For the organizational strategy to work, the local organization must obtain an appropriate resource base, technical assistance should use a mobilizer approach, and management capacity should be built by concentrating the effort on a few focal organizations rather than spreading it thinly among many. An explicit objective should be to strengthen a selected organization and prepare it to offer services to other rural groups. This has worked even when outside technical assistance was not involved.[17]

This need for concentrated effort parallels the need for concentrated authority necessary to deliver goods and services. But an organizational strategy for achieving sustainability does not profit from the use of performer technical assistance. Instead, teachers or mobilizers are more appropriate. This results partly from the uncertainty of the technologies available for capacity building.

Technological Strategies

Three approaches to technology may be derived from the IRD record. Each contributed to sustainability, or lack thereof, in a different way.

One approach has a wide following in the appropriate technology movement. In the IRD legacy, this has meant reducing dependence on external energy sources to lessen future foreign exchange requirements and the recurrent cost problem. For example, the use of animal traction for crop production in Botswana, Indonesia, the Philippines, Malawi, and Tanzania; of organic fertilizer to increase maize yields in Zaire, and of gravity- over pump-fed irrigation systems in Asia all represent this approach.

Relying as much as possible on local materials and resources is a sensible path to follow. When this approach was used in IRD, it did avoid, or lessen, some problems of achieving sustainability. In the Philippines, concrete roads were built to reduce maintenance and recurrent cost needs to a minimum.

But this was not the most common project assumption about the optimal technology for rural development. More widespread was the tendency to borrow pieces of green revolution technologies that required new varietal seeds, chemical fertilizers, and foreign exchange. The focus on sustaining these technologies was limited to three areas—continued subsidies for inputs, adaptive research, and strengthened links between research and extension. This amounted to refining and fine tuning a technological blueprint for increasing crop production.

Unfortunately, the blueprints were often faulty. Extension was commonly begun before there was a technology worthy of extension. This situation was especially true in dryland areas and in projects emphasizing rainfed crops. In Botswana, for example, the differences in rainfall within just a few kilometers could require different plowing and planting practices. In Tanzania, those technical packages that were successful succeeded only in the high rainfall areas. Similar limitations affected IRD projects in Liberia and Indonesia. But IRDP II in Jamaica showed the most persistent example of pushing poor technology.

Those projects involving irrigated rice production, such as the efforts in the Bicol, had more certain technologies. Nonetheless, there were usually weaknesses in the production technologies used in IRD. Both technical and managerial weaknesses were exaggerated when projects were based on the driving force of a pre-existing package of inputs; rigid designs were left helpless when the package did not work.

Occasionally, however, project strategies showed less faith in the power of these technologies. These strategies embodied a process approach as opposed to the blueprint approach.[18] This process approach is essentially a merging of institutional, organizational, and technological approaches into a perspective that measures success as the capacity to carry on and not as just immediate production gains.

Thus, when the uncertainty of social technologies and of rural environments is combined with a capacity-building view of rural development, a flexible, adaptive, learning-oriented approach is needed. This is called a process model.

The elements of a process model vary among individual programs—some are more process oriented than others. For instance, the Local Resource Management (LRM) Project in the Philippines, the Rural Sector Grant (RSG) in Botswana, the Arusha project in Tanzania, and PDP in Indonesia all contained process elements, even though their configurations varied. Nevertheless, general characteristics of a process orientation may be identified as:

- An emphasis on an extended, collaborative design process that builds a coalition of local actors committed to the project;
- A program-level effort using subproject learning laboratories;
- A design broken into discrete phases;
- An ability to provide flexible mixes of short-term technical assistance;
- An emphasis on the mobilizer model for long-term technical assistance;
- Frequent use of management workshops and action-oriented training among both staff and beneficiaries;
- A concern for participatory decision making and the use of temporary task forces or working groups instead of complete reliance on rigid management hierarchies;
- A reward system consistent with a learning orientation and an evaluation focus that goes beyond resource disbursements and production targets to emphasize the accumulation of local capacity;
- An applied research component with a learning repository located in a local institution;
- A redesign orientation, such as periodic revisions of project organization, project objectives, and job descriptions of project personnel; and
- A management and planning focus on the type and source of resources needed to continue benefit flows after the end of project funding, and the institutionalization of the capacity to provide them.

The process approach has been demonstrably more effective than the more rigid blueprint approach.[19] But is should not be used to justify management by abandonment.[20]

Indeed, the fear of inadequate accountability pervades discussion of the potential for using more process-oriented project models. Many pay lip service to the need to move away from blueprinting, but few will take the risks involved.

For the practice, as distinct from the theory, of rural development to move forward, design officers and donor agencies must be presented with a menu of workable options that allow flexibility within a framework of accountability.

Some options have been noted in earlier chapters. For example, RSG in Botswana used a rolling redesign process to produce annual budgetary blueprints within an evolutionary project design. Accountability was not lost. Instead, it was pushed forward into implementation so that resources could be rechanneled as learning occurred. This approach was different from the block grant image that leaps into many minds when the process model is mentioned.

Other projects also illustrate approaches that preserve various types and sequences of accountability. For example, the LRM project in the Philippines, the Training for Rural Development (TRD) Project in Tanzania, and the Agricultural Management (AGMAN) Project in Kenya all represent different types of process projects. LRM has an initial phase that is so flexible that it is nearly unguided in its attempt to build coalitions and identify local initiatives worthy of support in phase 2. TRD is training oriented with the range of target and resource institutions evolving with experience. AGMAN is two phased and designed with a flexible assistance fund used to act as a matchmaker for intermediary organizations in the agricultural sector and resource institutions that can help those organizations improve their performance. Illustrative activity budgets, redesign at the end of an initial phase, and periodic checks of direction changes are among the process characteristics that keep implementers accountable without tying them in red tape secured by rigid design targets.

Table 6 suggests a menu of project profiles to combine flexibility with accountability. The taxonomy is based on the perceived speed of project evolution and spending. The quickest is the elevator—the image that the term "process approach" often evokes. This model raises the fear of disbursement without control or of block grants that do not perform.

The escalator moves quickly, but it is more sensitive to accountability needs since it is based on rolling blueprints. RSG in Botswana typifies this model.

The third approach, the quick step, is a bit slower than the escalator. With two phases, it begins with a heavy reliance on outside assistance and moves toward reliance on local centers of excellence. Kenya's AGMAN project fits into this category.

The slow step approach begins with a lengthy coalition-building orientation during the first phase, which is essentially the design of phase 2. LRM in the Philippines is an example of this approach.

A key aspect of the process concept is the artificiality of the distinction between design and implementation. Rolling redesigns and subproject planning exercises are among the mechanisms used to cross this boundary. They also involve the same people in the entire process.

This is important because in blueprint-type projects there is no continuity between the people who plan and the people who execute projects. Designers do not have to live in the houses they build, and thus the focus of accountability is on controlling implementation excesses rather than on rectifying design mistakes. Process approaches try to overcome this weakness by incorporating

TABLE 6

Avoiding Blueprints: Alternative Process Strategies

Approach	Example	General Description of Design	Budget	Evaluation and Redesign	Subproject Role	Donor Role
Elevator Model	PVO Grants— Worldwide	Pool of money General guidelines, time frame, and implementing arrangements	High flexibility between categories Total based on illustrative activities	Annual In terms of guidelines Done internally	Varies	Provide money Provide TA as needed
Escalator Model	Rural Sector Grant—Botswana	Design has first year subprojects blueprinted with subsequent years showing budget total only	Each year's budget specified in detail at beginning of each year Total determined at beginning based on illustrative activities	Annual redesign process develops rolling blueprints Annual exercise evaluates previous year's subprojects	Total focus on supporting specific subprojects Implementation of subprojects through public sector	Participate in annual exercise Provide TA
Quick Step Model	Agricultural Management Project—Kenya	Phase I: • Blueprint for physical components • Rest as in elevator model • 2–3 year phase Phase II: • Budget total only • 5–8 years	TA set aside 20–25 percent flexible Total determined at beginning	Redesign exercise at end of Phase I Emphasis on learning in resource institutions	May act as matchmaker with evolving task groups and both public and private sector focus Temporary subprojects major focus for management assistance teams Intermediary organizations in agricultural sector are clients	Participate in design Redesign Participate in Phase I steering committee Provide TA

Approach	Example	General Description of Design	Budget	Evaluation and Redesign	Subproject Role	Donor Role
Slow Step Model	Local Resource Management Project – Philippines	Phase I: • 2–4 years • Project to design a program • Coalition building • Identify local initiatives Phase II: • 5–8 years • Implementation of program	Phase I flexible Phase II based on illustrative activities and determined at end of Phase I	Determined during Phase I Emphasis on continuous learning	Support of local initiatives major focus Community-based emphasis	Provide money Provide TA Approve Phase II Participate in Phase I working groups

design into implementation, and vice versa, in practical, operational ways rather than by making unrealistic appeals for less staff turnover in local bureaucracies. Process approaches, then, represent practical attempts to make things work.

Table 6 suggests the implications of the different models for budgetary flexibility, evaluation role, and other dimensions. But this is only a beginning. The IRD experience is that it is necessary to move beyond strategies that assume certain technologies that can be blueprinted. This move requires programming options that avoid simplistic blueprint versus process distinctions. The implementation experience indicates some preliminary directions, but much more remains to be done.

Summary

Financial, organizational, and policy constraints often impede local action leading to self-sustaining dynamics. Social and physical side effects can have a similar impact.

Institutional, organizational, and technological strategies were tried to overcome these constraints. One finding is that program-based rather than pure project-based efforts experienced more success. The need to build on established institutions permeated the entire IRD experience.

But no matter which approach was used, when technical assistance or capacity-building efforts were widely dispersed, little capacity was built and the prospects for long-term success plummeted. Similarly, when it was assumed that a project blueprint and a pre-existing package of technology provided a certain solution to local inadequacies, new problems overwhelmed management's capability to deal with them. This was especially true when the core technology did not involve irrigated rice production.

This exception was not just the result of technology, however. Local organizations need renewable resource bases, such as irrigation water or forestry preserves. Without this base, organizational strategies to attain sustainability usually fail.

While resource bases are built, a few focal organizations should be equipped to help others. The technical assistance approach for this effort should move away from performers toward mobilizers, organizational incentives should be scrutinized and adjusted, vertical linkages should be established with policy-level actors, and project designs should combine accountability with flexibility. Only then is it likely that issues of recurrent costs, capacity, and sustainability will receive serious attention.

Notes

1. P. M. Van Hekken and H.U.E. Thoden Van Velzen, *Land Scarcity and Rural Inequality in Tanzania: Some Case Studies from Rungwe District* (The Hague: Mouton, 1972), p. 47 and note 15, p. 124.

2. Irwin Levey et al., *Philippines—Rural Roads I and II*, AID Project Impact Evaluation Report no. 18, (Washington, DC: Agency for International Development, 1981).

3. World Bank, *Accelerated Development in SubSaharan Africa* (Washington, DC: The World Bank, 1981). This is often referred to as the Berg Report.

4. Robert Bates, *Markets and States in Tropical Africa: The Political Basis of Agricultural Policies* (Berkeley, CA: University of California Press, 1981).

5. Agency for International Development, "Project Evaluation Summary—Operation Mils Mopti (79-2)" (Washington, DC: Agency for International Development, 1979).

6. Marvin Miracle, "Evaluation of Some Aspects of Niger's Cereal Project," Project Evaluation Summary 79-5 (Washington, DC: Agency for International Development, 1979).

7. Albert O. Hirschman, *Development Projects Observed* (Washington, DC: The Brookings Institution, 1967).

8. Even though there is a common awareness of this fact, organizational and professional imperatives often lead to a glossing over of this issue, just as social soundness analyses neglect key project assumptions. The incentives are to move money, not to become involved with local realities. Recent trends such as policy dialogue make this situation even worse by deemphasizing even the rhetoric of collaboration.

9. This was true no matter which geographic region or country within which the project took place.

10. See *Tanzania Agricultural Policy* (Dar es Salaam: Ministry of Agriculture, 1983).

11. See David J. Gould, *Bureaucratic Corruption and Underdevelopment in the Third World: The Case of Zaire* (New York: Pergamon Press, 1980).

12. See Jennifer Bremer, "Building Institutional Capacity for Policy Analysis: An Alternative Approach to Sustainability," *Public Administration and Development* 4, no. 1 (1984): 1–13.

13. George Honadle, *Farmer Organization for Irrigation Water Management* (Washington, DC: Development Alternatives, Inc., 1978).

14. See Francis F. Korten, *Building National Capacity to Develop Water User Associations: Experience from the Philippines*, World Bank Staff Working Paper no. 528, 1982.

15. See Jerry VanSant and Peter F. Weisel, *Community Based Integrated Rural Development (CBIRD) in the Special Territory of Aceh, Indonesia*, IRD Field Report no. 4 (Washington, DC: Development Alternatives, Inc., 1979).

16. G. Honadle, *Fishing for Sustainability: The Role of Capacity Building in Development Administration*, IRD Working Paper no. 8 (Washington, DC: Development Alternatives, Inc., 1981).

17. See Chapter 2, notes 26–28.

18. This dichotomy and the preference for the process model have become an orthodoxy among many development specialists. This is unfortunate. Delivering goods and services and using performer types of technical assistance are sometimes necessary components of good strategies, and they should not be denigrated when they are needed. The problem is the imbalance, not the existence of these elements.

19. See Donald R. Mickelwait et al., *Personnel Requirements for Project Development in East and Southern Africa* (Washington, DC: Development Alternatives, Inc., 1977).

20. George Honadle and Jay Rosengard make this argument—process does not mean unfocused. See "Putting 'Projectized' Development in Perspective," *Public Administration and Development* 4, no. 3 (1983): 299–305.

CHAPTER FIVE

Reflections and Projections

The field of rural development is in a healthy state of ferment. New ideas are emerging from field experience and practitioners are drawing on the lessons assembled by academics. Moreover, a breed of practitioner-scholar is in the making—with its heritage drawn from throughout the globe. Africans, Asians, Europeans, North Americans, and South Americans are all contributing to a new awareness of the bonds linking humankind and the need to tap multiple sources of inspiration for development strategies.

In the midst of this activity, however, there remain bastions of thought and power that cling to narrow interpretations of rural development and its outcomes. Micro processes such as project development procedures, the organization of development programs, the approach to technical assistance, and the style of management found in a particular initiative all reflect the interpretation integral to that initiative. This can have a profound effect since micro processes often determine the effectiveness of strategic options—thus, the importance of implementation.

The preceding examination of implementation indicated that it is a loosely tangled collection of micro processes—team dynamics, interpersonal relations, administrative procedures, logistical details, and political agendas loom large as they combine in numerous ways to influence the experience. This interpretation emphasizes the need to understand the peculiarities of specific circumstances before plunging ahead with broad agendas that may not be appropriate. At the same time, however, implementation patterns are informative in a wide range of situations.

Institutional development and sustainability concerns highlight the somewhat counterintuitive and contradictory nature of development management. Clusters of elements, not single factors, produce success. Implementation follows a winding path, not a straight line, from where things are to project objectives. There is no shortcut. The twists and turns of multiple objectives, informal processes, contradictory roles, and shared risk are necessary. Thus the lessons from the experience will be equally intertwined and each one must be seen in relation to the others.

This chapter concludes this book by emphasizing general lessons of the IRD implementation experience and suggesting their implications for future development assistance. Both pitfalls and promising pathways are discussed.

Pitfalls of Experience

Learning starts by realizing and admitting that a mistake was made, and then not repeating it. Learning also takes place by repeating a practice that appears to have worked. But when it is not understood why something did or did not work, it is much harder to predict whether different circumstances will produce different results.

Explanations for the minutiae of implementation often fall on deaf ears because they stress details that do not interest planners, economists, and policy makers, who are more attracted to the power and prestige attached to the overall situation. But without an appreciation for what happens after policies are declared and plans set in motion, grand designs are likely to be unrealized and the means for attaining them unsustained. Until this situation is rectified, development efforts will continue to encounter the same traps and pitfalls as in the past.

The IRD experience highlights some problems and myths that plague the development enterprise in general. It also suggests some ways to avoid repeating past mistakes.

Rhetoric and Resources

One lesson that jumps out from the IRD experience is the need to match resources to objectives. A project manager cannot build organizations with long-term viability when the project budget is devoted to the short-run installation of physical infrastructure.

Much of the failure of IRD may be directly attributed to this mismatch between resources and rhetoric. Mixed signals lead directly to mismanagement. Not only were the resources committed to developing the infrastructure, but the focus of evaluation teams was also on the compilation of progress toward physical production targets. Admittedly, these were easiest to assess. Nevertheless, the result tended to twist attention away from the key issue of sustainability.

Essentially, this approach represented the equation of artifacts and development. Since projects were short-term, time-bound activities, efforts to be funded had to fit into the project mode. Physical infrastructure emerged a clear winner. The loser, however, was the developing economy. Ignoring the need for organizational capacity building and applying resources primarily toward immediate physical production served to exaggerate the misconceptions already blocking sustainable development and delayed the creation of the needed organizational infrastructure. Great amounts of money and talent were channeled toward the physical dimension, while the behavioral side (which needs more time and effort) was slighted. Thus, the imbalance was not just between rhetoric and resources; it was also between needs and commitments.

Adding the rhetoric of equity and self-reliance to a construction budget is not the way to design better development processes. Nor is it a way to help managers. Until budgets and schedules reflect a commitment to long-term organizational learning, the mismatch between rhetoric and resources will remain, and sustainable development will continue to be elusive.

Organization and Function

Just as rhetoric and resources were often out of kilter, so too, organizations and functions were commonly mismatched. Project components that could have benefited from the use of a temporary unit were often housed in line agencies, whereas those requiring a long-term presence were placed in project management units (PMUs).

Jamaican and Liberian projects provide particularly obvious examples of this phenomenon. Both fragmented authority by having a road-building component in the Ministry of Public Works and a production and agricultural services component in a PMU. The second component was designed to stimulate local action through satellite organizations, provide inputs, strengthen marketing services, engage in research and extension, and promote basic changes. Such a mission requires a long-term presence in a stable institution. But the projects were organized to use temporary PMUs for this job.

At the same time, a job that was appropriate for a PMU was given to a permanent institution. Feeder road construction could have been successfully accomplished by a temporary task force. Instead, resources for this effort were channeled into a line ministry—Public Works.

Thus, these projects not only fragmented authority at a stage calling for concentration, but they also placed responsibilities in organizations ill suited to perform them. Even if there had not been contextual and technical problems with these projects, they would most likely have failed because their organizations were inappropriate.

Development Decision Making

The 1980s have brought a period of structural adjustment programs throughout the developing world. Global recession has squeezed the south hard, and the bureaucratic inefficiency that could be tolerated during a period of growth has become a far heavier burden.

Yet remedies do not recognize the key role of administrative performance. Prescriptions by the International Monetary Fund typically assume that a few changes in policies and prices will restore good management and restabilize economic performance. But the record suggests that this attitude is naive. Until basic patterns of decision making are changed, adjustments will continue to be unsustainable.

The issue of decision making comprises three dimensions—formality, delegation, and politics. Formality and delegation have been discussed repeatedly throughout this book. Politics has also been noted, but it must be re-emphasized. Although it is fashionable to present politics as an opportunity rather than just as an obstacle to implementation, and to cast technocratic imperatives as somewhat less critical, the IRD experience encourages a different view.

Political development requires an acceptance of technical parameters as a guide for action—storage facilities belong in production areas, not in the president's isolated village; hazardous waste cleanup should be based on the seriousness of the pollution, not on the political preference of the local residents. And political development is a prerequisite for sustainability.

This implies that organizational decisions cannot be dominated by actors whose expertise is based solely on their political position. This does not mean that dams should be built if they are technically feasible, but it does mean that they should not be built if they are not technically appropriate. But in countries in which political parties hold undue sway over daily implementation decisions, sustainability concerns too often yield to considerations of who gets what now. Many problems of IRD implementation and the poor record of sustainability can be reduced to this factor.

Contemporary Myths

The mismatch between rhetoric and resources and the difficulty of developmental decision making may be seen as reflections of a pair of myths that permeate the field of international development. The first issue reflects the myth of the technical fix. The second represents the myth of the noble peasant.

The myth of the technical fix is based on the idea that development is simply a technical problem. The myth promotes the perception that solutions to the development puzzle are known, and the reasons that they are not applied result solely from bureaucratic ineptitude and political shortsightedness. The answer to poor performance, then, is to bypass the bureaucratic obstacle course and let the experts do their job. Project management units (PMUs), the infrastructure complex, and faith in green revolution technologies all typify this approach.

The myth of the noble peasant accepts the idea that development is simply a socio-political problem. Since rural villagers, according to this myth, know how to do it, the answer is to get out of their way and let them get on with the job. This attitude promotes the idea that local participation is the panacea for elite aggrandizement and bureaucratic bungling, and that the rural poor are the only legitimate inheritors of development benefits.

In IRD, the technical fix appeared as rigid project plans based on faith in the driving power of a production technology. With the exception of irrigated rice, however, the faith was unwarranted, and even there the technology was not a sufficient force to make the jump from resource application to sustained development.

A newer version of this perspective is in danger of arising—a preoccupation with microcomputers as a solution to ineffective management and decision making. Given problems of data storage, retrieval, and analysis in many bureaucratic settings, microcomputers do offer an appealing alternative to the stacks of dusty file folders that crowd many offices in developing countries.[1]

But microcomputers do not manage data. They can only assist properly trained staff to reduce the task to manageable proportions. Moveover, microcomputers are most useful for jobs in which data categories are relatively discrete, such as demographic analysis and municipal financial management. The development of simple software packages for wider applications may contribute to development management, but a microcomputer cannot compensate for an ill-conceived information strategy or management process. The technical fix appears in many seductive forms, and although new equipment may facilitate some management functions, the presence of solid state artifacts cannot be equated with organizational capacity.

The noble peasant myth appeared in IRD through projects designed to eliminate the roles of middlemen, entrepreneurs, and financial intermediaries and to replace them with peasant cooperatives. Thus, there was a bias against individual private merchants and money lenders. Sometimes it was justified because they were predatory. But this was usually an oversimplification. From Tanzania to Thailand, small-scale urban entrepreneurs often served the downtrodden—those with the resources to buy only a pack of cigarettes helped those with enough resources to purchase only a single cigarette.

Rural experience is consistent, too. Salaried government or parastatal employees may be reluctant to gather the produce of isolated farms or unable to extend credit, whereas self-employed private traders will do so. This can be crucial for the survival of marginal farmers.[2] Yet the myth of the noble peasant blinds observers to these facts, and the blinders can be most difficult to remove when the traders belong to an unpopular or nonindigenous ethnic group.

But the noble merchant should not become the new light that blinds us to social inequity and non-Western values in developing country environments. The present emphasis by donors on the private sector is derived largely from Western ideological roots, rather than from development theory or empirical data. The result is a mixture of good and bad ideas. At the same time, bureaucrats rush to implement projects requiring knowledge and skills historically absent in donor agencies, implementing agencies in host countries, and many rural environments. If the style of implementation is marked by rigidity and dogmatism, the new emphasis will repeat the failings of IRD.

When private sector institutions can play an appropriate role, they should be used. For example, efforts to increase off-farm employment through the development of small-scale enterprises represent a promising opportunity, and many manufacturing and assembling firms have an interest in reliable local supplies of components or raw materials. These firms may play a helpful role even in training and assistance to small-scale entrepreneurs, improving quality control and production scheduling. But a rush into the private domain may reinforce the problems of inequitable growth while ignoring the lessons learned from the experience gained in the public sector. In many locations, these public bureaucracies offer the only practical means to address many needs of rural villagers. To abandon these bureaucracies for ideological reasons would be a grave error. A better approach is to determine a local mix of public or private initiative and internal or process capacity that can achieve sustained development.

Both the technical fix and the noble peasant perspective must be rejected as distorted and simplistic. Neither gadget fixations nor romantic visions have proved adequate for the design and implementation of rural development. Instead, they have handed down a legacy of performer models, bypass strategies, and blueprints gone awry. Fortunately, however, the IRD experience also contains some signs pointing toward promising pathways.

Promising Pathways

Lessons from IRD are based on success and on mistakes. When things did not work, the experience provided guidance about what to avoid or, in some cases, how to do it better next time. When results were forthcoming, the experience demonstrated what can be done or why certain paths are more fruitful than others in specific circumstances.

In either event, IRD does suggest some routes that should be taken in the future. This section discusses them in the form of practices to encourage or questions to ask.

Local Leadership

Effective leadership at the local level is a critical factor in implementing and sustaining development initiatives. Informal leaders drawn from the community who have strong personal and family ties tend to act on a perceived community interest.[3] And yet these leaders may lack the skills required for some organizational tasks, or they may be captive to local interest groups unsympathetic to development efforts. These potential problems must be weighed against the leaders' ability to provide traditional legitimacy, knowledge of informal processes, and capacity to mobilize community support.

- Projects should build on pre-existing leadership.

Community organizations may benefit greatly from the expertise, influence, energy, and commitment of local leaders, provided that they will share decision making. Indeed, even when local groups are formed to serve the interests or defend the rights of the most disadvantaged, effective leadership is likely to come from those who are relatively more advantaged and closely allied with the local power structure.

The link between local leadership and outside leadership is also a key element in success. Use of informal channels and a view of management as external negotiation rather than formalized communication and internal supervision characterized good leaders in all situations. Assistance strategies should build on local leadership without abdicating responsibility for providing help to develop that leadership.

- Accountability should be broad based.

Traditional leaders are more likely to act in ways that support local interests if they are held accountable to a broad constituency, regardless of their group of origin. This accountability may be defined by both locally and more centrally determined norms and standards. It will be more effectively enforced if incentives and sanctions are applied not only from above, but also from below.

Participatory Management

The more project staff are allowed to participate in planning and managing a project for which they bear some responsibility, the more their own attitudes and performance are likely to support project objectives. Nonetheless, in practice, delegation of significant responsibility or resource control to rural staff is rare. Perhaps the greatest constraints to this delegation are the structures, systems, and norms of the bureaucracies responsible for rural development administration, combined with a tradition of centralized decision making. This tradition is often rooted in history, politics, and culture, but is usually reinforced by the widely held perception of senior officials that lower-level staff are inadequate to accomplish much on their own. But the real reasons for low staff productivity may relate instead to terms of service, living or working conditions, and poor supervision. These conditions and their consequences suggest that not having enough qualified staff—a frequently cited development constraint—may reflect failures in the management and use of available personnel.

- Low-level staff capabilities should be built through shared decision making.

Failures stem not only from misperceptions regarding the potential of low-level personnel but also from fears of relinquishing power and authority. These misperceptions and fears tend to become self-fulfilling prophecies. When staff are not allowed to participate in decisions affecting their work, their motivation and sense of worth decline. The resulting desultory performance then becomes the rationale for their continued exclusion from participation in decisions about activities they must carry out.

- Introducing a participatory system must be a long-term strategy, not a temporary measure.

Because it is different, a long-term participatory system may confront forces that try to compel compliance with more established methods. The commitment to change must therefore be demonstrated by the willingness of higher-level officials to share access to resources and opportunities.

- The rules must be made clear.

Explicit guidelines that define the boundaries of participation are needed. The absence of these guidelines may cause staff to misunderstand how they should participate, what results may be expected from the process, or what limits there may be to the use of their ideas. In particular, the difference between making a decision and being involved in decision making must be understood. Effective management often requires that one person have the ultimate responsibility for key decisions. Encouraging the participation of others does not mean relinquishing responsibility to them. Instead, it means sharing a common development process with them.

Open Management

Related to the issue of participatory management is that of open management. Open management refers to a quality of communication and coordination both within the management structure of a project or agency and between their staff and the beneficiaries with whom they interact. Open management is the result of both formal and informal processes.

- Structured mechanisms such as committees, liaison offices, task forces, and beneficiary meetings must be supplemented by informal communications and contacts as well as by staff attitudes that encourage responsiveness to beneficiary interests and concerns.

Most central to the concept and functioning of open management is access to information in usable and understandable form by those who have a legitimate interest in that information. This access is particularly important when local groups act on behalf of the entire community or use its resources.

- Open management can help ensure accountability by local leaders to the people whose interests they supposedly represent.

In light of the many bureaucratic constraints to open management, attention must be given to staff development as a way to build appropriate practices within public and private organizations. Sustainability and open-management strategies should be developed and applied at bureaucratic, beneficiary, and project levels to create concentrated supportive activity.

Possible strategies for staff development include a career system in which young people start in rural areas and are ensured of advancement for meritorious service in those areas; special allowances and other incentives for service in hardship posts and especially isolated rural projects; pre-entry and in-service training of technical and professional personnel; emphasis on action training using administrative skills oriented toward participatory methods such as joint planning, team building, negotiating, and listening; and evaluating and rewarding staff on the basis of local results, not completed activities or funds expended. A combination of structural and process elements will be needed.

Open management may be difficult to install, but once it has taken hold, it quickly demonstrates its value in any setting. It is a key to the flexible, learning-oriented processes that characterize successful development. Moreover, reorienting existing institutions toward open management creates a climate that supports working through channels rather than attempting to bypass them.

Avoiding Bypass

One common approach to IRD has been to bypass local institutions through the use of organizational avoidance mechanisms, such as a PMU; design elements, such as displacing merchants with cooperative societies; or behavioral practices, such as the performer model of technical assistance. The inadequacy of these approaches strongly suggests that future rural development programs should try to work through existing institutions and enhance their capabilities.

But for such a shift to occur, a procedural prerequisite may be necessary. The practice of project development by international donors may, itself, obstruct the shift.

Design of projects is a major donor activity. There are numerous reasons for this. First, since a donor is primarily an investor and since it must be shown that monies are wisely invested, design skills are highly rewarded. In fact, personal success within these agencies is measured more by the bureaucrat's success rate in getting new projects approved than by the effective implementation of those projects.

Design in this context, then, emphasizes packaging for approval within the donor institution rather than initiating processes that enhance the capacities of recipient institutions. As a result, project design is typically characterized by the short-term performer model of technical assistance (TA) and by a focus on the design document rather than the design process.

The design document is all important. To produce it, two short-term teams are often used. The first team conducts a feasibility study. The second team is activated after the recipient country has reacted to the first study. It questions the original design in light of comments and changes in the local situation, refines it, and then packages it for the journey through the donor-approval maze. During the second exercise, the final design is also negotiated with the host government. When these projects fail, blame is generally attributed to poor management rather than to the inadequacy of the design process itself.

Even when donors do tinker with design procedures, they seldom hit the mark. In the mid-1970s, for example, the United States Agency for International Development (AID) reduced its design process from three stages and three documents to two. This reduction was to have shortened the delays between a project idea and the beginning of implementation. This, according to the logic, should have resulted in better designs because fewer environmental changes would have made the original strategy less obsolete.

But performance was little affected. The problem was misdiagnosed. What should have been questioned was the performer and product emphases of the design process and the blueprint role of the design document. The focus on delays continued to legitimize a bypass approach that treats the design process as distinct from capacity building.

Aggravating this separation is the treatment of administrative capacity as though it were a residual category. Only when implementation problems loom large, and when it is often too late, does capacity become a focal topic. Thus, the typical design practice does not support capacity building. Instead, it is a head-in-the-sand strategy that handicaps implementers, emphasizes performer TA, and may be inherently antithetical to development and capacity building.

Alternative design processes and alternative ways to use a design must be explored. Accountability requirements, donor mandates, and the fact that designs represent a negotiated and formal agreement between donors and recipients all dictate a central role for design. The challenge, however, is to develop design approaches and configurations that support learning processes resulting in enhanced local capacities and initiatives.

- Projects adopting a bypass approach should be penalized within the donor approval process.

The bias should be to use and enhance existing institutions. Administrative capacity should be a central concern. Its assessment should result from lengthy collaborative designs rather than from quick visits by outsiders charged with design responsibility. A red flag should appear whenever a proposal suggests creating a new organization, and technical assistance strategies should be thoroughly scrutinized to make sure they are not excessively performer oriented.

This does not mean that new organizations should never be created, nor does it mean that performers should never be used. They have their place, but care should be taken to avoid using them when they are inappropriate.

- Projects should be designed to be more flexible, adaptive, and evolutionary.

Dichotomous thinking about blueprint versus process is obstructing the ability to experiment with innovative approaches to project phasing, budgeting, and management. In Chapter 4, multiple characteristics of process designs and alternative approaches to project configuration and accountability were identified. Attempts to test these approaches and develop new ones should be encouraged.

- The project design process should be revamped to emphasize building coalitions and capacities en route to a design.

Project designs could emerge from program-assembling exercises averaging about two years. A major emphasis during this period would be to identify local initiatives that could be supported and to field test new ideas. A project design exercise might be funded as a project itself—a first stage in a long-term commitment.

This approach is also no panacea, but it does offer promise as a way to proceed beyond the present deadlocked state of the art in development programming. Experiments could be tried initially as an adjunct to the present operating pattern. In AID, for example, project development and support funds already provide a track that could be expanded and strengthened. For institutional bypass and project blueprinting to be dropped as the normal field approach, however, they must be made more difficult within the donor agencies.

Concentrating Capacity

The advent of AID's New Directions mandate in 1973 was a major departure in development strategy from the approach of the previous decade. The targeted focus on the poor heralded a new breed of project. IRD was one strain in that new breed.

The poverty focus recognized that overly concentrated wealth imposed political and economic burdens on developing governments by limiting markets, encouraging the flight of capital, perpetuating corrupt bureaucratic practices, reinforcing poverty pockets, promoting unproductive use of scarce capital, and supporting political instability. But the equity orientation also had its own costs. The New Directions approach tried to get benefits directly to the rural poor, but this led to dispersed collections of subproject activities that exhausted capacity rather than enhanced it.

To avoid repeating this undesirable situation, future development efforts should address some issues that have been clarified by the mixed results of New Directions programs. They include the following:

- Actors in the project development process must examine tradeoffs between concentrating effort and running the risk that predators will gather the majority of benefits *versus* dispersing effort and running the risk that no capacities will be built to carry on after the project ends.

This tradeoff is often a real one, and there is no easy answer. But if the issue is not examined, the mistakes of the past will repeat themselves.

- Programs should build a local capacity to provide technical assistance services.

Program designs, styles of technical assistance, training strategies, and even financial management procedures should all be selected with this issue in mind. Intervention components and objectives should make it a central concern and not a peripheral element. A focus on project inheritance should dominate designs.

The strengthening of local resource institutions to provide long-term, post-project technical support should be integral to that focus.

- Designers should focus on the most appropriate local organizations.

Pre-existing capacity to perform activities and deliver services to particular target groups is a factor that will guide the choice of which organization to help. Prior legitimacy and established resource control are desirable characteristics. An important factor to guide selection is also an organization's posture toward open management. The compatibility between the requirements of open management and the present operating mode suggests the potential performance capability of a specific organization.

- Technical assistance must be kept on track so that the local organization increases its performance.

Agreement on the behavioral model for technical assistance, and supervision and evaluations supporting the mobilizer and teacher approaches, will be required to avoid the pitfalls of an overemphasis on performer technical assistance. Training strategies and the use of short-term technical assistance should be supportive. Both internal and process capacity should be monitored and enhanced, with the mix of the two depending on the local situation. At the same time, attitudes should avoid falling into the development machismo trap. The strategy should use and focus on the five process elements (collaborative style, learning focus, risk sharing, multiple levels, and demonstration) as well as the two structural elements (resource base and incentives) characteristic of successful capacity building.

A decision about where to concentrate capacity-building efforts will have political ramifications. This is unavoidable. The decision may be both hard and sensitive, but it must be made. Especially as resources become even more limited, the need to concentrate will grow stronger. The IRD experience indicates that widely scattered investments produce only diluted capacity and little in the way of sustained benefit flows.

Planning for Sustainability

Sustainability is not automatically a by-product of development projects. It must receive serious attention from project inception through termination. Among the considerations that should guide planning and management attention are the following:

- What benefits are to be sustained?

A careful distinction should be made between temporary, project-related outputs and intended long-term benefit flows.

- What resources will be required to fund long-term benefit flows?

Will project systems be self-supporting (for example, a credit system whose administrative costs are supported by interest income), or will a permanent subsidy be required? It is particularly important to distinguish capital costs from recurrent costs in making this analysis. If a local organization is used, its access to a renewable natural resource base and its certainty of control of that base are key elements to be examined.

- If external resources will be required, what will be their source?

Assuming termination of donor funding, a secure and predictable source of long-term subsidy should be identified before the subsidized activity begins.

- Do projected benefits justify the investment of external resources in light of realistic constraints and opportunity costs?

Projects often represent funds in search of activities. Continuation, in contrast, represents activities in competition for funds. For good reason, the host government may view many activities as a poor investment, even if they were once approved for donor funding.

- Does the administrative capacity exist or is it being developed to maintain essential systems for the continuation of benefits?

Organizational capacity, leadership, history, and resource control are key issues.

- Are permanent aspects of service delivery being institutionalized in government or private sector structures?

If so, are new administrative resources required (such as extension agents, credit staff, or technical assistance), or are there already slack resources in the system, that is, existing staff who function at less than full capacity?

- How much of the requirement for both financial and administrative inputs can be undertaken locally?

Local inputs, if soundly based, reduce dependency, increase dependability and predictability, and serve the interests of local control.

- Is each project component housed in an organization that is appropriate for the tasks to be performed?

The concentration of authority when needed, the sharing of authority when needed, the requirement for a long or brief presence, incentives for performance, the requirements of individual tasks and the interrelationships among tasks, and a focus on local action must all be considered. The need for someone to perform the deputy role must also be examined.

- What measures will be taken to link staff action to local action and focus on post-project inheritance?

The structuring of staff incentives, technical assistance, evaluations, leadership style and attention, recruitments, satellite organizations, policy settings, private-public sector linkages and various contextual factors will all need attention during the design process. Particular attention to pre-existing patterns of informal interactions is called for. Consideration of how the project can build on positive patterns and foster local initiative can make the difference between failure and success.

These considerations have implications for which activities are incorporated into development projects as well as how they are organized. One particular implication is for the scale of project interventions. Projects implemented on a small scale can frequently take advantage of slack resources in the system. That is, existing administrative and extension staff who are functioning at less than full capacity may be used in expanded project activities — their numbers need not be increased if their efficiency is improved. Up to this point, concern for sustained resource commitment is minimal; beyond this point, when a commitment must be made for additional finances, the concern is substantially increased. Furthermore, local government reluctance to fund recurrent costs in place of more visible capital investments makes it more likely that small-scale efforts will not overtax slack resources.

This perspective may also be applied to project components. Although an effort may be large, if subprojects are small and self-contained, the most appropriate ones may continue to provide benefits after project termination.

Final Lessons

This review of IRD implementation experience was not conducted as a typical piece of research. Instead, it resulted from attempting to assist field staff with the job of rural development. The research agenda was secondary to the action agenda.

Similarly, the purpose was practical — to codify and expand the knowledge base so that it could be used to improve performance in the field. At the same time, the immersion in field realities generated implications for theoretical and training undertakings.

Academic Implications

Although a development project is intended to influence and change its environment, organization theory stresses the effect an environment has on an organization.[4] In reflecting back on the field experience recorded in this account, one is struck by the extraordinary accuracy of the academic literature. Although the penetration of the project varied with the way it was organized, there was a pattern of environmental domination of projects. PMUs had similar problems in different countries, but all the projects in a particular country shared characteristics and mirrored local class structures and organizational dynamics.

Organization is partly a way to regulate the interactions between a group of people and external actors. Thus, the organization of a project will influence those interactions. In fact, the battle to choose an organization will be partly political because different groups will have an interest in guiding those interactions in different directions. This view also is supported in the literature, suggesting that organization theory has much to offer practitioners of development administration.

But this account also raises questions that are not addressed by the theory. The literature does focus on the issue of management with multiple objectives. But the IRD lessons include the fact that the sequential objectives of development programs contain contradictions of an organizational nature—the overall goal requires contradictory means. The literature does not deal with this issue. Organization design for a sequence of contradictory needs opens a new set of issues, and it recasts the terms of ongoing debates.

One ongoing debate has emerged on the issue of whether Western management theory is built on universal precepts or whether development management requires the use of forms and practices that are found only within particular cultural and historical settings.[5] According to the experience base presented here, both are right.

The IRD record suggests that some universal organizing strategies, such as a matrix organization, do not work when supportive contextual factors are absent. Some management styles, however, do appear to be universally effective, such as open management and the use of informal mechanisms for decision making. Their exact nature varies by place, but the style is consistently successful. All successful development managers used informal approaches to build coalitions before they embarked on any new directions. But the informal vehicles that they used varied by setting. Village fiestas in the Philippines, church groups in Liberia, and society meetings in Jamaica all offered situations in which members of competing organizations could work out differences in neutral arenas. Effective leaders took advantage of the particular opportunities available in the local environment. Thus, the general practice of informal negotiation was a universal characteristic of success, but its implementation style and mechanisms had to be context-specific to work.

When the leader was a project manager, informal negotiation with notables was facilitated by the presence of a deputy who was concerned with the internal project management. The same was true of TA team leaders and program-level officials, suggesting universal applicability of this factor. Similarly, temporary project organizations were effective at service delivery and ineffective at sustaining project-initiated efforts.

Open management was also consistent in its ability to perform. Although relatively open cultures such as in the Philippines might be expected to accept this approach to hierarchy and accountability, more closed ones would be expected to reject it. Yet even the relatively formal and closed societies found in Indonesia welcomed it. Posted decisions and public budgets appeal to a desire to hold leaders accountable that transcends culture.

But for this approach to work, it must be taken seriously. The difficulty of introducing these practices in a country such as Zaire might be far more costly than in less-resistant settings, but experience elsewhere suggests it might not be impossible. The means of introduction would be contextural, but the practice could promote improvement in all the settings studied.

The universalist-contextualist presentation focuses attention on the match between mechanisms and settings. But this is not the only type of organizational mismatch responsible for explaining the poor performance of development managers. The analytic framework used in this book indicates that the mismatch between mechanisms and objectives is equally important.

Orthodox management science does offer sound guidance for delivering goods and services. Clear objectives, lines of authority, agreed-on procedures, collegial trust, control of resources, and other common attributes of good management can make a difference. But generating local action and sustaining benefit flows are objectives that fall outside the domain of formalistic Western management theory. The best organizations for service delivery are seldom appropriate for the later stages in the implementation model. Thus, the organization theory concept of task environment, which lumps objectives and settings together, is inadequate for dealing with development management in its entirety. Universalistic management science is a useful starting point for the first linkage in the model, but the contextual mappers may possess the tools required to forge the second and third linkages.[6]

Organization design seems to make a difference: the problem of implementing a local organization strategy varies among PMUs, private voluntary organizations, subnational units, or lead line agencies, and the chance that recurrent costs will be picked up is related to organizational placement and the decisions that accompany it. Similarly, different organizational approaches place different demands on managers; yet a few basic approaches yield results in all settings. Thus, some answers exist to theoretical issues, but many questions remain.

One remaining issue concerns the rules of evidence. That is, in dealing with subjective and interpretive dimensions of human action, such as management and management capacity, what rules may be used to judge the quality of the evidence presented?

Observers of organizational phenomena often disagree over what has been witnessed or the meaning of the different occurrences. For example, one writer concluded, based on Asian experience, that there is no relationship between the use of PERT and similar techniques and organizational capacity.[7] Another, based on African experience, suggested that these methods, when combined with a forced time-bound focus, were instrumental in raising organizational capacity.[8] What are the rules of evidence, the appropriate time frame, and the proof of performance?

These issues are all relevant to this book. The evidence presented here is not a typical research report with correlations between independent and dependent variables specified. Instead, the approach has attempted to place the experience of involvement, with a flavor of management processes, into a conceptual framework that allows sense to be made from a collection of loosely comparable incidents. Although to some this approach will seem less rigorous than the traditional mode, to others its significance will lie in its emergence from action rather than just observation. To others, the value will lie in its attempt to keep the sense of management process in the forefront. Indeed, this difference of perspective is the essence of the question of the rules of evidence.

These issues also belong in the forefront of professional training programs. Training in rural development administration cannot afford the narrowness or luxury of a focus on only traditional social science research methods or the organization and management literature. Environment influences the operation of organizations, and area studies are needed to equip students to appreciate these dynamics. Resource bases are critical for organizational survival, and a merging of management and technical knowledge, such as that promised by the field of social forestry, is necessary to educate professionals capable of improving local capacities. Informal management styles are most productive, and students should be instructed in their creation and use. Research skills should include the techniques of new departures, such as rapid appraisal, to blend engagement and reflection in ways that build capacity and lead toward sustainability. Effective mobilizers, not just competent performers, are needed.

But theoretical, methodological, and training considerations are secondary. The primary concern of this book is with the practical implications of the IRD experience.

Practical Implications

In Chapter 4, inappropriate policies were identified as an important barrier to the achievement of sustainability. Among the most common are policy imperfections that keep farm-gate prices artificially low to serve the interest of urban populations and parastatal marketing organizations.

To many economists, however, this situation is not one among many constraints; instead, it is the key constraint.[9] The orthodoxy of the 1980s is get the price right, cut back the parastatals, unleash the private sector, and let development bloom. The assumptions are that macroincentives, such as prices, can bring about the management capacity needed to keep production up and that the risk of abandoning present institutional arrangements is less than the diseconomy of maintaining them, especially in Africa.

But the IRD experience suggests that the situation is more complex. The capability to manage a transition to the research and extension programs necessary for long-run adoption and success is lacking from many settings. Furthermore, the carrying of personnel, the assumption of the debts, and the distribution of the assets of dissolved marketing boards or production parastatals are not merely technical details to be resolved by low-level civil servants. Instead, they are politically charged issues that invite political confrontation.[10] Resolving these issues in healthy economies with resource reserves would be difficult. Doing so in the fragile developing country settings of the mid-1980s requires highly skilled strategic managers.

The problem, then, is not just to announce new prices and abolish public sector organizations. It is also to select among a range of institutional configurations to promote sustainable development those that contain acceptable transition risks, and then to manage the transition process, while recognizing that uncertain knowledge and evolving objectives will make the original configuration become obsolete. The policy problem is therefore actually an institutional problem with an implementation dimension.

Implementation is as central to the success of policy reform as it is to the sustainability of IRD. In fact, even if IRD is abandoned as a major approach to development, an enduring lesson that emerges from the approach is the importance of organization and management. Induced development is a management-intensive process and the selection of effective microlevel processes is necessary to ensure the viability of macro-level strategies.

Recognizing this central role of human action through organizational channels, the IRD experience offers testimony to both strengths and weaknesses in past development strategies. First, it indicates that resource mobilization and management are key requirements for success. Harnessing the power of a natural resource, such as water for irrigation, is a necessary base for self-reliant development. When efforts are not rooted in an exploitable energy source, they are likely to falter and die. Development must be based on real resources and not just on dogmatic dreams. Unless rural populations receive the tools to tame their surroundings, they will remain hapless victims of both natural and social forces.

Second, the donor-driven and project-fueled drive to bypass local institutions poses a serious threat to sustained development. There is little evidence that temporary PMUs can build local institutional capacities. IRD efforts that were program based and housed in established institutions appear to be far more able to build local capacity to survive in the long run. In large, diverse countries, this approach usually implies working through a subnational government body. In smaller, less heterogeneous places, a national-level body may be a more likely host. After all, the differences between Indonesia and Botswana, for example, are real, and the varied resources, histories, and scales cannot be compressed into a single organizational model. At the same time, a common theme does emerge—build on what exists instead of seeking a nonexistent *tabula rasa*.

Third, decentralized, flexible, informal decision making must be allowed. Development cannot be dictated. It is a struggle that must be embraced willingly and a journey that follows a winding path with unpredictable obstacles and opportunities. Overly bureaucratic procedures induce underdevelopment. Development is performance promotion, not bureaucracy building. Societies and organizations that cannot accept this fact are destined to founder. Fortuitous resource endowments, such as precious minerals or valuable fuels, may delay the day of reckoning, but eventually that day must come. Rigid national plans, bureaucratic blueprints, and donor dogmas must yield to a style of leadership that stimulates creative capacity rather than stifles it. Although this poses a threat to many who hold power, the opposite threatens sustained development and self-reliance.

Fourth, a fatal flaw in IRD in general is a lack of humility. Attempts to install stockaded enclaves of comprehensively planned new worlds in a wilderness of underdevelopment were naive and arrogant. The belief that the key factors inhibiting development could be discerned by project designers who could then provide an integrated attack, and the expectation that the purity of the enclave could somehow transform its environment to mirror itself, were highly unrealistic.

But this view must also be qualified. The common perception that IRD is comprehensive is not supported by the field experience. Although the range of project profiles is wide, IRD usually emphasizes agricultural production and physical infrastructure, with a few other components tacked on. The naiveté, then, applies less to technical omniscience and more to the expectation that an enclave could induce new, sustainable dynamics.

Fifth, when the transition from starter motor to main engine does take place, it is usually a result of a fortuitous conflux of supporting circumstances as much as developers' intentions. These circumstances include world market trends and political interest on the part of powerful actors. But if adequate management capacity is not in place and able to capitalize on those circumstances, the result is likely to be failure. Thus, the approach to implementation and the degree of flexibility do make a difference. Good implementation does not guarantee success, but poor implementation is sufficient to block sustainability.

Sixth, sustainability does not emerge from quick stabs at the symptoms of major problems. Instead, it requires long-term commitments that build on experience and apply steadily increasing pressure on the causes of problems. Projects are often terminated exactly when they have brought about a few preconditions necessary for their success. But shifting fads, personnel turnover, and the desire to begin new efforts make sustained follow-through unlikely. Few bureaucracies reward those who successfully persist with others' ideas. Instead, ownership and credit accrue to those who are the architects of new departures. The resulting changing project emphases alternately raise and dash local expectations at a rapid pace and create a doubting environment that makes a long-run focus much more difficult to achieve.

Seventh, organization and management are central elements of development. Not only are they important in determining the problems encountered during implementation and the ability to overcome those problems, but they are also a key to what happens after an intervention is completed. Management capability is a major ingredient in sustaining what was begun. Success requires a concerted push to make the strengthening of organizational capacity the central tenet of development programming. The emphasis must shift away from attention to the donor project cycle toward the post-project inheritance and the ability of organizations to use that inheritance as the basis for further initiatives.

Eighth, the tendency to look at organizational assets, rather than at performance and the resource base and incentive systems that surround the assets, is a common failing of IRD. As a result, naive training strategies and subsidy programs contribute little to the post-project viability of local organizations. In retrospect, it seems to be common sense to deal with the core of the problem, but what appears to be common sense does not appear as common practice.

This situation is complicated by a focus on individuals—whether they are managers, entrepreneurs, or beneficiaries—as the determinants of success and the inheritors of capacity. It is tempting to project the image of a prominent individual onto the character of an organization. However, the leap from individual action to group behavior can drastically change the image.

For example, a fly-casting fisherman on the shore of a Scottish lake becomes a factory ship in the mid-Atlantic or a spear fisherman in a dugout canoe becomes a fleet of motorized canoes with nets. Although the individual picture is romantic, the organizational reality may not meet the ideal. This is one aspect of the problem encountered by those who have attempted to specify and measure the dimensions of capacity—measures of individual cognitive skills are inadequate indicators of organizational strength or weakness. Although the factory ship may be staffed by bright and skilled individuals, ethnic rivalries, inequitable division of the catch, lack of equipment, and numerous other factors can thwart the use of skills. Thus, measurement requires an examination of organizational attributes rather than just an aggregation of individual ones, and effective capacity building requires an organizational focus.

Ninth, successful development management is based on informal processes that build and use obligation and exchange relationships grounded in the local environment. The use of imported management systems has little relation to project success, and analyses that focus on formal systems invariably miss the major dynamics of implementation. This also suggests that sustainability requires the augmentation of informal dynamics that push toward post-project initiatives consistent with project objectives. Sustainability, then, is less the maintenance of project assets than the enhancement of local capacities.

Tenth, there are basic micro-level contradictions inherent to rural development. They manifest themselves in organizational mechanisms that coexist uneasily, in sequential objectives that require different principal actors and management styles, in simultaneous desires to use and ignore situational politics, and in concurrent recognition of the primacy of informal individual leadership behavior and the need to institutionalize formally this behavior so that good starts do not collapse. Resolving these contradictions requires, at minimum, appropriate organization, phased efforts, flexible designs, transition planning, skilled strategic managers, and a focus on post-project inheritance.

Finally, the IRD experience suggests that there are no algorithms for success. There are necessary ingredients, but no sure recipes, ideologies of the moment notwithstanding. There are basic contradictions within the process of induced development, and no single organizational form is effective at all stages in the process. Approaches must be evolutionary and adaptive. Organizations or individuals who desire guaranteed outcomes, specified solutions, or lock-step procedures should not enter the domain of rural development or capacity building because this arena is permeated with anxiety, uncertainty, contradictions, and a need to experiment.

Whether these lessons are incorporated into the actions of donors, recipients, elites, or peasants does not rest just on the quality of development strategies or whether they are integrated or sectoral, project or program, social learning or infrastructure, bureaucratic reorientation or peasant production, or public or private sector. Instead, it rests primarily on the seriousness given to the development enterprise. Development is essentially a creative and artistic social endeavor, not a technical procedure or a political dictate. But until development is the primary agenda, implementation will seldom follow a course that leads to sustainability. The challenge is to steer for that course.

Notes

1. Michael Morfit, Donald R. Mickelwait, Robinson Tarigan, and Jerry VanSant, *Toward an Improved PDP Information System* (Washington, DC: Development Alternatives, Inc., 1982).

2. N. K. Nyanteng and G. J. VanApeldoorn, *The Farmer and the Marketing of Foodstuffs*, Technical Publication no. 19 (Legon: Institute of Statistical, Social, and Economic Research, University of Ghana, 1971).

3. The key role of leadership is often ignored because it is seen as a nonreplicable factor that eludes analysts, planners, and donor designers.

4. See, for example, James D. Thompson, *Organizations in Action* (New York: McGraw Hill, 1967); Goran Hyden, *Efficiency versus Distribution in East African Cooperatives: A Study in Organizational Conflict* (Nairobi, Kenya: East African Literature Bureau, 1973).

5. The universalist position is represented by David K. Leonard, *Reaching the Peasant Farmer: Organization Theory and Practice in Kenya* (Chicago: University of Chicago Press, 1977). The contextualist position is found in the writings of Jon R. Moris. See *Managing Induced Rural Development* (Bloomington, IN: Indiana University, International Development Institute, 1981).

6. A potential source of theoretical assistance is to be found in exchange theory.

7. David Korten, "Community Organization and Rural Development: A Learning Approach," *Public Administration Review* 40, no. 5 (1980): 480–511.

8. George Honadle, *Fishing for Sustainability: The Role of Capacity Building in Development Administration*, IRD Working Paper no. 8 (Washington, DC: Development Alternatives, Inc., June 1981).

9. World Bank, *Accelerated Development in SubSaharan Africa* (Washington, DC: The World Bank, 1981). This is also known as the Berg Report.

10. Robert Bates, *Markets and States in Tropical Africa: The Political Basis of Agricultural Policies* (Berkeley, CA: University of California Press, 1981).

APPENDIX A

Project on the Organization and Administration
of Integrated Rural Development:
Field Visits

Location	Project or Activity	Purpose of Visit	Date(s)
Asia			
Indonesia	Save the Children Federation Community Based IRD (CBIRD) Project	Assessment of Capacity-building Strategies	9/79
	Provincial Area Development Program	Assessment of Institutional Development Strategies	8/80–9/80, 2/81
Thailand	Policy Analysis	Review of Thai Government Development Strategies and Programs	5/79–6/79
Nepal	Rural Area Development –Rapti Zone Project	Information System Development	12/79–4/80
Pakistan	On-Farm Water Management Project	Institution-building and Information System Assistance	10/81, 2/82–3/82
Philippines	Libmanan-Cabusao Project (IAD I)	Water Users Workshop	6/81–7/81
	Bula-Minalabac Project (IAD II)	Organizational Development Workshops for Project Staff	4/79, 10/79, 5/81–6/81
	Local Resource Management Project	Design Assistance	10/81
	Rainfed Resource Development Project	Design Assistance	10/81–11/81
	Bicol Integrated Area Development Project III (Buhi-Lalo)	Project Assessment	5/81–6/81
Africa			
Tanzania	Maasai Range Management Project	Analysis of Organizational Factors Affecting Technical Assistance and Performance	5/79–6/79
Botswana	Rural Sector Study	Assessment of IRD Project Implementation	4/79

	Rural Sector Grant	Implementation Review and Subproject Assessment	10/78, 11/80, 2/81– 3/81, 7/82– 8/82, 2/83– 3/83, 3/84
Liberia	Lofa County Integrated Agricultural Develop- ment Project	Management Workshop and Other Management Assistance	2/79– 3/79, 3/80, 11/83
Sudan	Abyei Rural Develop- ment Project	Status Review	1/81– 2/81
Niger	Niamey Productivity Project	Training	10/81– 12/84
Cameroon	Mandara Area Development Project	Institutional Analysis	8/80
Middle East			
Egypt	Sectoral Strategy	Management and Train- ing for Decentralized Projects	12/80, 8/81
Tunisia	Central Tunisia Development Authority	Project Management Training and Assistance	11/82
Latin America and Caribbean			
Honduras	Small Farmers Technology Project	Assistance with Information and Coordination Issues	1/79, 6/79
Jamaica	Second Integrated Rural Development Project	Management Skills Development and Support Activities	3/80, 5/80, 11/80, 3/81
Colombia	Integrated Rural Development Program (DRI)	Review of Organizational and Administrative Issues	10/80– 11/80
Panama	Sona Integrated Rural Development Project	Design Assistance	5/81– 6/81
Ecuador	Rural Development Secretariat	Information System and Organizational Assistance	3/81– 4/81, 6/81– 7/81

Characteristics of 21 USAID-Assisted Integrated Rural Development Projects

Country	Project Name and AID Project Number	Implementation Dates	Organizational Placement	Components	Donor Funding (million $)	Host Country Contribution (million $)	Location
Bolivia	Subtropical Lands Development Project (511-0346 & 511-0514)	1975–82	Lead-line agency	Ag. extension, research & input supply, road construction, potable water, health, colonization	9.7	5.1	Chane-Piray, San Julian areas
Colombia	Community Based Integrated Rural Development (514-0210)	1976–80	PMU	Ag. extension/farmer training, credit, road construction and improvement, health, nutrition, education and school construction, community development	1.0	1.1	Sibundoy, Guadalupe, Sumapaz
Haiti	Gros Morne Rural Development (521-0081)	1977–80	PMU	Credit, health, community development	0.13	n.a.	Gros Morne
Haiti	HACHO (Haitian American Community Help Organization (521-0061))	1972–79	PMU	Ag. extension & research, road construction, health, nutrition, education, community development	6.6	0.9	Northwest Province
Indonesia	Community Based Integrated Rural Development (497-0240)	1976–80	PMU	Ag. extension, credit, bridge construction, potable water, sanitation, electrification, health, nutrition, education, cooperative development, rural industry	2.0	n.a.	Tangse and Lam Teuba, Aceh Province

Country	Project Name and AID Project Number	Implementation Dates	Organizational Placement	Components	Donor Funding (million $)	Host Country Contribution (million $)	Location
Indonesia	Luwu Area Development and Transmigration Project (497-0038)	1976–82	Lead-line agency	Ag. extension, road construction, irrigation system construction, colonization, health	15.0	45.0	District of Luwu, island of Sulawesi
Indonesia	Provincial Area Development Program (497-0264)	1978–85	Subnational government agencies	Ag. extension, research & input supply, credit, rural industry promotion	6.0	4.3	Eight Provinces
Jamaica	Second Integrated Rural Development Project (532-0046)	1977–82	PMU	Ag. extension & research, road construction and improvement, soil conservation/reforestation, potable water, electrification, cooperative development	15.0	11.2	Pindars Rivers & Two Meetings Watersheds
Kenya	Vihiga/Hamisi Special Rural Development Program (615-0147)	1970–78	National IRD agency	Ag. extension & research, credit, livestock and range management, road construction and improvement, education, rural industry, socioeconomic research	1.8	0.25	Vihiga & Hamisi Administrative Divisions
Lesotho	Thaba Bosiu Rural Development Project (632-0031)	1973–78	PMU	Ag. extension, research & input supply, credit, livestock & range management, marketing, road construction and improvement, soil and water conservation/reforestation, socioeconomic research	8.4	1.4	Maseru

APPENDIX B (Continued)

Country	Project Name and AID Project Number	Implementation Dates	Organizational Placement	Components	Donor Funding (million $)	Host Country Contribution (million $)	Location
Liberia	Upper Lofa County Agricultural Development Project (669-0022)	1976–81	PMU	Ag. extension, research & input supply, credit, road construction and improvement, cooperative development	11.0	7.0	Northern part or Lofa County
Mali	Operation Mils-Mopti (688-0202)	1976–83	Subnational government agency	Ag. extension, research & input supply, marketing, road construction and improvement, potable water, rural industry	21.5	4.3	Mopti District
Mauritania	Integrated Rural Development (Guidimaka) (682-0201)	1977–83	PMU	Ag. extension & research, livestock and range management, soil and water conservation/reforestation, cooperative development	6.0	1.7	Guidimaka Region
Nicaragua	INVIERNO (524-0118)	1976–	National IRD agency	Ag. extension, credit, marketing, community development	12.0	18.0	Central Interior & Central Pacific Regions
Philippines	Bicol Integrated Rural Development Program (492-0303/0260/0275/0310/0289)	1974–85	Lead-line agency	Ag. extension, research & input supply, credit, land reform, road construction, & improvement, electrification, health, nutrition	29.6	58.6	Bicol Region, Southeastern Luzon
Sudan	Abyei Rural Development Project (650-0025)	1979–81	PMU	Ag. extension & research, potable water, health, communications, cooperative development	1.3	1.8	Abyei District, South Kordofan Province

Country	Project Name and AID Project Number	Implementation Dates	Organizational Placement	Components	Donor Funding (million $)	Host Country Contribution (million $)	Location
Tanzania	Arusha Planning and Village Development Project (621-0143)	1978–82	Subnational government agency	Ag. extension & research, credit, road construction, & improvement, potable water, rural industry, regional planning	5.5	16.0	Arusha Region
Tunisia	Siliana Rural Development (664-0307)	1977–81	Subnational government agency	Livestock and range management, road construction & improvement, potable water, health, community development	1.6	n.a.	Makthar & Rohia Delegations, Siliana Province
Upper Volta	Eastern ORD Integrated Rural Development (686-0201)	1975–80	Subnational government agency	Ag. extension & research, credit, marketing, road construction & improvement, socioeconomic research	4.8	1.0	Eastern Region of Upper Volta
Yemen Arab Republic	Community Based Integrated Rural Development (279-0031)	1978–81	PMU	Ag. extension & research, road construction & improvement, potable water, health, nutrition, community development	1.5	0.3	Mahweit
Zaire	North Shaba Maize Production Project (660-0016)	1977–81	PMU	Ag. extension, research & input supply, marketing, road construction & improvement, cooperative development, rural industry, socioeconomic research	13.4	9.6	North Shaba Region

INDEX